Churchy

Churchy

THE REAL LIFE ADVENTURES OF A WIFE, MOM, AND PRIEST

by

SARAH CONDON

A Mockingbird Publication

MOCKINGBIRD

Editing by David Zahl.
Cover by Tom Martin.
Published 2016 by Mockingbird Ministries.

ISBN-13: 9780990792789
ISBN-10: 0990792781

For Josh,
I'm in Paris with you

And for Neil and Annie,
our babies

ACKNOWLEDGEMENTS

Thanks to my mother, who never shied away from the hard things. And thanks to my father, who taught me how to write about them. If you want to make the world a better place, then raise your daughter to be bold.

For my brother Aaron, who loves story and laughter.

I cannot thank my grandmothers enough. For Elizabeth, who taught me about Jesus. And in memory of Lois, who taught me how to dress for church. Lois, you were right. I was too mouthy for most men. But I found the one that would marry me.

For Dr. Ted Ownby who taught me that the South lives in the sin of her own making.

For Paul Zahl, who taught me about the relentless redemption of Christ.

For my friends of many years who love me more than I deserve: Lindsay, Rychelle, Emily, Clint, Hawley.

There are so many church communities that have made this book possible.

My life changed in the pews of Calvary St. George's Church in New York City. Jacob and Melina Smith have both been dear friends and preachers of the Gospel for Josh and for me. We are grateful for you.

St. Martin's Episcopal Church has been the most supportive place I have ever worked. I'll never have another boss as kind as Russ Levenson. It's just not possible. Thank you to everyone who lets me yammer loudly in their offices. Which is everyone.

Holy Spirit Episcopal Church and School has seen our family through so much. And they have done it with generosity and love. I especially want to thank the teachers and volunteers who have cared for our children. You made this book possible.

In seminary, they tell you never to become friends with parishioners. This is total bullhockey. Melissa and Kim, you showed up and shaved my daughter's head when we found out she had a terrible case of lice. Karen, you are a constant encourager. Ellen, thank you for letting our little family sit with your little family, Sunday after Sunday.

The blessed community, indeed.

Mockingbird saved my life. They also saved this book. Thank you to the hours of editing and emailing you offered me. David Zahl is a prince among men. Thank you to Scott Jones, Lindsey Hepler, Margaret Pope, CJ Green, and Ethan Richardson. I get to write alongside some remarkable women. Stephanie Phillips, Charlotte Getz, and Carrie Willard, I praise God for your voices.

Neil and Annie, when you read this someday, you should know that being your Mama makes me happier than anything on the planet. You are my precious peanuts. And you always will be.

Finally, thank you to sweet Josh. You put up with so much, show up for so much, and love us so much. I cannot believe you belong to us and we belong to you.

TABLE OF CONTENTS

INTRODUCTION

"Are you guys wearing KKK hoods?!"

I started college at a small liberal arts school in Santa Fe, New Mexico. Upon arrival, I affixed several family photos to the wall of my dorm room. After about a week of classes, one of my friends uncomfortably pointed to a photograph of me and my brother and asked the above question.

"Nope," I snapped back, "those are acolyte robes. We were at church."

Like most of my Mississippi peers, I grew up in a household where church was a mandatory activity. But unlike the committed Southern Baptists and dutiful Presbyterians of my childhood, I couldn't have told you exactly why. We did not read the Bible at home. No one asked me if I wanted a Promise Ring at fourteen. Bibles were for keeping family records, and sex was for college. This was the sage wisdom of my childhood.

When my mother would wake us up at 7:30AM to get ready for the early service, I would complain to her that our churchgoing made little sense. She appeared to lack the fervor of her peers. My parents never lectured us on salvation or moral behavior. Our church attendance never had much to do with the way my parents voted or who they kept as friends. What was the point? Why were we even going? In response to my complaints Mom would simply say, "We take you to church every Sunday so you have something to fall back on when life gets hard."

Life did get hard. Not because something dramatic happened but because I am a person in the world. I didn't last very long at that college in Santa Fe because I am more straight and narrow than I would like to admit. I ended up at The University of Mississippi. It took me two years to have more than one friend. And all the while, I kept going to church.

Much to both my parents' and my surprise, I felt called to ordained ministry. Which just goes to show, the harder you pray for your child to be a pastor, the more likely you are to end up with a mixologist. My advice for raising children to be Christian is to take them to church and not talk about it too much on the ride home.

Life is hard now for other reasons. I married a wonderful guy named Josh who also happens to be a person in the world. So we love each other unequivocally and also fight about things like how fast he drives or the lack of mayonnaise in my egg salad. We have two children, Neil and Annie. And while they are the best thing that has ever happened in the history of the planet, they are not the fashion accessories that the Kardashian family promised me they would be.

Josh and I are both Episcopal priests. But most Sundays, you can find me in the pew with our children. On occasion, I stand behind an altar and celebrate communion. All of it is wonderful, altar and pew. Yet despite how much our life sounds like a liturgical Hallmark movie, you'll find in the following pages that we are just as smelly, angry, and broken as you are. And you will see that church is a place I cannot seem to stay away from.

Someone asked me recently what I hope my children gain from regular church attendance. "Oh, that's easy," I laughed. "That their Mama really, really needs Jesus."

Often, when my children are noisily barreling down the aisles for communion, I remind myself that it's a *good* thing how comfortable they are in church. In truth, we are there so much that it must feel like home to them. At home you let it all hang out. You are loud and insistent, loving and sad, joyful and funny. Through the beautiful language of the church, my children are learning that Jesus loves them. They are hearing about their own sin and God's forgiveness. Also of great importance, our weekly church habit offers them something to fall back on when life gets hard.

Originally, I wanted to call this book *Prodigal Daughter.* Whenever I read that parable, I am struck by how much I resemble *both* of the siblings involved. I am the daughter who runs away from God, looking for the world to bring me happiness. Yet, I am also the daughter who thrives on righteousness and responsibility (Luke 15: 11-32).

It turns out that somebody already wrote a book called *Prodigal Daughter.* In fact, several people have written books by that title. Some of them are written by parents who refer to their children as "prodigal" (Seems a little judgmental to me. Does that make the parents God?). Others appear to be bonnet-rippers, which is to say, chaste erotica. And if there is anything I have not been in my life, it is chaste. My expertise lies elsewhere.

Fortunately, as St. Paul wrote, "Jesus came into the world to save sinners, of whom I am the worst." Incidentally, *I Am the Worst* would have been an excellent title for my book. We went with *Churchy* because it sounds like a nightclub and because it is undeniably true.

The truth is I am churchy to my core and proud of it. I need the sacraments, I long for the liturgy, and, to be totally honest, I enjoy weak coffee. Mostly though, I am churchy because I need to hear the Gospel preached week in and week out. I have never understood believing in Jesus and not going to church. I don't judge the choice. I just figure non-churchgoing Christians must have a better memory than I do. Because I forget about the unrelenting grace of God all the time. I have to hear about it with alarming regularity.

I suppose that's a long-winded way of saying that the real title of this book should be *Churchy Prodigal Daughter Who Is the Worst*. Which is a mouthful, sure, but at least it beats *The Adventures of a Chaste Klan Girl*.

1

ACCEPTING REALITY
(ONE SUSHI ROLL AT A TIME)

A timeline:

> *First year of marriage:* You try to claim your autonomy by declaring that all housework should be equal.

> *Years two through four of marriage:* No one does any housework. Your kitchen looks like a *Hoarders* episode.

> *Year six:* You have a baby. Babies cannot live in filth. You both start cleaning. Haphazardly.

> *Year seven:* You realize how nice it is to live in a somewhat clean house. You start reading mom blogs about cleaning.

> *Year eight:* You discover that cleaning is kind of enjoyable. You are still reluctant to admit this fact. After all, your personhood is at stake.

> *Year nine:* You give up. You like cleaning. And you're home more. So, it makes sense, dammit.

> *Year ten:* You no longer fantasize about knifing
> your beloved while scrubbing toilets. If that's
> not sanctification, I don't know what is.

I keep a lot of women friends in my life who have kids a few years older than my own. While they may still be in the trenches of motherhood, they have at least managed to pop their heads up now and then to glance at the enemy fire.

As God's providence would have it, the same week one of my wise mom friends explained to me, "Sarah, you are either a lice family or a butt worm family," I found out we are the former.[1]

Upon receiving the horrifying and humiliating "we found a live bug in your child's hair" phone call from the school, I began to grapple with my new reality. I left work. I went to the drugstore. I bought the lower shelf in a section that should be marked "Everything Itches." Then I went home to my husband who had dutifully picked up both of our infested children in the middle of a work day. Everyone stared at me like, "*Well*, what should we do?"

I realized, in that moment, I was running the Great Delousing Fest of Casa Condon. And, like in the Irish Potato Famine and the Civil War, the lady of the house needed to be on the front lines, because, for whatever reason, this diagnosis fell under the purview marked

---

1. Yes, butt worms are a thing. They have a more scientific name. But do you really want to know more than that?

"Mama." Unlike taking out the trash, cleaning up dog vomit, and making grilled cheese sandwiches, everyone clearly thought I knew what to do.

I leapt into action. I suggested we all eat something before this whole process started (potato chips and chicken salad—I run a real tight ship). I googled everything ("*Can* lice be in beards?"). I figured out what could be washed and what needed to be dipped in bleached acid.

Now, I want to be very clear with you that this is not at all how I would have responded our first year of marriage. Absolutely not. If we had encountered such a crisis early in our marriage, I would have been very clear that this sounded like a *you* problem and not like a *we* problem. Thank God, we never had lice in our first year of marriage, but we did face our own demons. And I rarely faced them well.

It is important to note here that my husband and I got married, as Johnny Cash would say, "in a fever." There were loads of things we did not know about one another. This caused issues for longer than I care to admit. Perhaps our biggest crisis occurred when I learned that my husband is allergic to salmon. It was almost a deal-breaker.

> Husband: Oh yeah, we can't order that sushi roll. I'm allergic to salmon.

> Me: WHAT? How did I not know that? Salmon is my favorite food! This is terrible for me! Are you sure?!

9

Husband: Yes, I'm sure. I swell up and have a hard time breathing.

Me: You've just had bad salmon. We should just try it one more time. No one is actually allergic to salmon.

Husband: I mean, okay. I'll try it. (With great reluctance, consumes one sushi roll.)

Thus began a night of deciding whether to walk to the closest ER on the East Side of Manhattan or to just keep having Josh chug Benadryl. To be honest, I do not remember feeling particularly worried about him. I definitely did not feel like I had done anything wrong. He was clearly having an allergic reaction to salmon, and that seemed like a *him* problem.

I had long been of the belief that marriage should be an institution founded on fairness. It did not seem fair that I had unknowingly married this Salmon Bubble Boy. Had he intentionally hidden this malady in our premarital counseling? Surely he didn't expect me to go without? How was I supposed to live out my autonomy as an Independent Woman who loves Rainbow Rolls? None of this was fair.

In retrospect, that night could have gone differently. I *could* have just seen his allergy to God's finest sea creation as a quirky new thing I was learning about my husband. I *could* have filed it away under "Important Things to Remember About Josh." And even after I forced him to tempt asphyxia, I *could* have been more tender with him. I certainly *could* have apologized.

But I did not do any of these things. Because it was easier to think of myself as a woman liberated from the role of "wife" than it was to think of myself as a co-signer in a covenant of sickness and health. It was more comfortable to stand on the firm ground of fair-mindedness than it was to sit in the bathroom with him while he threw up. I missed out on so much trust and love that night simply because I wanted to feel good about myself and my decisions.

Too often, the laws of autonomy do us in. They allow us to self-justify and categorize. These laws quickly become unintentional barriers to real love. Sacrificial love. Love that does not measure who last unloaded the dishwasher. Love that does not blame or persecute. Love that is, in fact, patient and kind.

I tell you this story because I want it to be clear that love, especially married love, is an evolution. Two things happened in my life that began to change the way I viewed my role in marriage. First, I realized that being the chore-tallying, salmon-pushing wife was not making me happy. I had often worried that if I loved without rules and boundaries, then I would be taken advantage of. If I did not remark on how many times I had done specific domestic duties, then perhaps my husband would forget how valuable I was. I had forgotten that he did not marry me because I do things well. He married me because he loves me.

The second event that altered my heart was the arrival of our first baby. Our son almost completely destroyed my need for fairness and autonomy. Babies don't care about fair. I had grand plans about how much my husband would take care of the baby. We would "split up" the duties and make certain our efforts never overlapped. All of that fell apart the first night we brought our tiny son home from the hospital. After hours of being awake with a very upset newborn, I took the baby and told my husband to go to sleep. I sat on the couch and positioned our son on my stomach almost exactly where I thought my womb was. He fell asleep in seconds. I was the only person in the universe our baby wanted. He didn't give a hoot about all the egalitarian childrearing plans his mother had in mind.

This is not some call for women to embrace a caricature of a bygone era's housewife. You do not have to like cooking meals every night. I am not suggesting we all will want to clean toilets. I write this merely as an encouragement to fall in love with the life you have been given. Risk everything for your role as wife and mother. Put to flight your long-held notions of fairness. Let the boundaries around your heart fall away.

If I had wanted a marriage founded on fairness, I was stupid to get married in a church. In church, we often talk of our marriages being founded in Christ. And Jesus was terrible at encouraging equitable relationships with good boundaries. Just ask those people who worked all day in the vineyard. Or the ninety-nine lambs that got left behind while he searched for the lost one. Or even the disciples who felt they had rightfully earned their place at the front of the heavenly queue.

By God's grace, I have started to see my place in the household as something set apart and sacred. Could I document a balanced chore chart and insist that my husband "do his part"? Could I insist he put the kids to bed because I've been home with them all day? Would he fall into the lines I demanded of him? Sure. But our household is undeniably calmer and sweeter if I step into my God-given roles. I can claim injustice and unfairness for the tasks that seem to fall under "Mother" or "Married," or I can simply skip those unhelpful thoughts and step into the remarkable role of being a wife and a mama.

My point here is not to burden these vocations. Only to name them as such. Too often we think we have randomly landed ourselves in this time and space, but nothing could be further from the truth. God, in all of his mercy, chose this man to be my husband and these children to be my babies. If I am too busy scorekeeping and rule-making, I will deny myself the intimacy and relationship that I was truly made for. In John Baillie's remarkable devotional, *A Diary of Private Prayer*, he writes of our lives:

> Almighty God, who of Thine infinite wisdom
> has ordained that I should live my life within these narrow bounds of time and circum-

stance, let me now go forth into the world with
a brave and trustful heart.[2]

Let us not waste too much time trying to deny the reality of our lives. Life is incredibly short. Mothers die at thirty-five years old every single day. Children pass from being little and needy to being self-sufficient adults in almost an instant. This moment, with its bottomless piles of laundry and little faces asking me what's for dinner, is undeniably precious. I would do well to accept my place in it. Salmon allergy and all.

2. I discovered this incredible little devotional book from J. David Hawkins' *The Useful Sinner*, which relates the story of Hawkins' own marriage falling apart and coming back together after his adultery. Baillie's book is crucial to his healing.

2

LOW ANTHROPOLOGY
IS MY LOVE LANGUAGE

Walk into any big-box bookstore in this country, and you'll find a table of well-designed paperbacks that promise to unlock your hidden talents and awaken you to the power that lies within. Hilariously, these books are typically found in the section marked "Spirituality/Religion." One book after another tells us we are *powerful* and *positive* and *limitless* creatures.

Unfortunately, that is not the kind of book you are currently holding. Don't get me wrong, I have mornings when it feels as though I can "do all things" through Sarah's own self-driven neurosis that strengthens her. But we all know that is not how the Bible verse goes. Most days, my children, my husband, and our dog have all punctured my sham before I've had my second cup of coffee.

I know what you must be thinking, "How can I invite Sarah over for my next dinner party? She is so cheerful!"

When I served as a hospital chaplain, I remember being tempted to take a swing at a patient over this very issue. The patient began to evangelize to me (not how this relationship normally works) about a television preacher who told her she would get better if she "got positive." Normally, I would have let this kind of thing slide. People tell themselves some desperate stuff in the confines of a hospital room.

But I distinctly remember being moody and very pregnant so I said, "Being positive all the time sounds hard and like it might not fix everything." To which this patient replied in a slightly patronizing tone, "I feel sorry for *you*." To which I replied somewhat more aggressively, "I FEEL SORRY FOR YOU." It was not my best day of ministry.

Often, like the patient I verbally accosted, people accuse me of being negative and depressing. They tell me human beings are inherently good. That we are capable of anything that we "envision" for ourselves. I wish I could believe human beings possessed a default button for moral behavior. One glance at the evening news tells a very different story. When it comes to what we want in this world, I suspect most of us picture a gigantic house and Scrooge McDuck piles of money.

To be clear, I do not want to be negative for negativity's sake. I just have what theologians call a "low anthropology." Which is to say, my theology tells me humanity is a clown parade of jackwagons. This is the crux of why we need Jesus to save us. He didn't come because we are all good vibes and motives. He came because we have always been a sinsick ship of fools.

For a long time, people have heard a kind of Bootstraps Gospel in our churches. We are told if we can just be good and moral creatures, if we can do enough outreach work, if we can pray our daily devotional every morning at 6AM, and if we can smile at everyone who is sad, *then* our righteousness will shine like the morning sun. Preachers have stood in pulpits and offered a vacant Christianity. They have preached that we must do our part in order for Jesus to do his. Church people will negate what we know about persecuted Christians in the world (they must not be praying hard enough) or the number of faithful Christians who cannot escape their demons (again, not praying hard enough) all for the sake of believing it is our devotion and do-gooderism that saves us.

Outside of the church, we hear this optimistic or "high anthropology" narrative everywhere. People want to tell you how to be better, faster, and stronger without acknowledging the innate failure and darkness fundamental to human nature. We will ignore the news, our struggling neighbor, and any honest discomfort in our lives all for the sake of having "good energy." We must be shiny new pennies all the while denying the crevices we inhabit.

In America, we do not actually know how immoral and self-serving we have the potential to become. We are not, generally speaking, a desperate people. We are not persecuted and tortured. We do not know how we would respond to a Holocaust or to ethnic cleansing. But if our fellow human beings are any indication, I suspect we would hide in our homes and hope the horror would leave us unscathed.

Rest assured, no amount of positive thinking would pull us out of such depravity and sickness. Certainly, there are those few people who are willing to sacrifice their lives for the sake of others. And we all hope we would do the same. But those people are heroes because they are the exceptions. While we would all like to assume that we would be the Dietrich Bonhoeffer or Martin Luther King, Jr. of our generation, the odds are against us.

Part of me *wants* to believe in our capacity for goodness. I want to think human beings strive for excellence and are on the fast, or even slow, train to self-betterment. But we all know life is two steps forward, and then forty-five dramatic pitfalls back. I hold fast to grudges and deny my baptismal promises daily. I utter expletives out loud while writing someone a pleasant email. And while I realize this whole thing may sound like the confession of my mental break, I know I am not alone. None of us are reliable directors of our salvation.

Whether we like it or not, a low anthropology exemplifies the reality of human nature juxtaposed with the perfection of Christ. If he did not come to save us from ourselves, then what did he come for? To be a teacher? A prophet? A community organizer? He was an elusive teacher at best, a failed and crucified prophet, and the world's least organized community organizer. Too often theologians want to place these labels on Jesus because none of us want to face the horror of just how much we need him.

Jesus swam in the violent and hateful waters of our anthropology so he could pull us out and save us from ourselves. He was perfection in the midst of chaos and cruelty. Perfect love in the face of abject hate. Our low anthropology is the precise compliment to his high Christology. If you ever find yourself in a church that tells you otherwise, you should run screaming out of the pew.

Some years ago, I walked into a church in desperate need of a good word. A dear friend had died violently, and I was hoping the preacher could give me something, anything, to console me. In the Scripture for that morning, Jesus had appeared before his friends after being crucified. He came to offer them comfort and the promise of the Holy Spirit. "This is exactly what I need," I remember thinking to myself. Then the preacher stood in the pulpit and offered next to nothing.

He relayed a story about an old car he had and how much the car had been through (you know, like wrecks) and how much he loved his car and how his car had scars just like Jesus. "We all have scars," he insisted, "just like the scars of Jesus. Hopefully that's a comfort to you."

I just sat there and thought, "If that's all you got, then

I'm screwed." I need Jesus to be Jesus. I need his scars to be more than just *like* mine, I need them to *redeem* mine. His scars are the sins of humanity made manifest onto his very being. My scars are the sin that will kill me.

A low anthropology is an honest one; it calls a thing, a thing. Admittedly, this drive to see ourselves as #worldchangers comes from a well-intentioned place, at least partly. In a world hammered daily by pain and torment, we are all desperately on the lookout for some hope. We intrinsically need faith in something. If it isn't God, then the onus falls on our shoulders—and eventually life wears us down to the bone. If you think a low anthropology is bleak, just try to imagine gathering up comfort all by yourself. Try to imagine a way to survive such profound aloneness. Cancer and addiction and depression are not illnesses we can positive-think our way out of. Envy and judgment and anger are not sins we can simply turn over a moral leaf and change.

Hoping in ourselves and our ability to create good vibes (or positive energy or whatever New Agey physics term we're currently co-opting), is like thinking we can make chocolate cupcakes out of horse manure. Sure, for a few seconds, maybe even a minute or two, we can sit in a dark room and believe humanity is bootstrapping its way into a collective #bestlifenow. But then we talk to another human being who wants something from us we do not want to give. Or we pause to reflect on our bosses, parents, in-laws, and/or spouses and just how much they can frustrate us. And there it is again, good old-fashioned sin and pride making itself known.

There is an odd gap between our perceived self-optimism and the reality of who we are which can smack us in the face at the most inopportune times. In truth, it is the same gap between who we tell Jesus we are on Sunday mornings in worship and who Jesus knows we are an hour earlier when we are yelling at everyone to get dressed for church. It is the difference between lying to ourselves about how great we are and being honest about just how much we need a savior.

There is another gap in my life that brings me undeniable relief from myself. It happens for about twenty-five seconds most Sunday mornings. Each time I receive the bread and wine of communion, all of my sin meets all of God's forgiveness. Inevitably, I have approached the rail burdened by myself. I have snapped at my children for crawling under pews. Or judged other people's children for crawling under pews. I have been anxious about my young son's clothing choices while also wondering why the acolyte doesn't have her hair pulled back. It turns out that my low anthropology follows me especially closely into the pews of Sunday morning worship. Whatever sin is swimming in my head on Saturday night is still treading water on Sunday mornings. After all, church isn't a transgression-free zone. In all likelihood, I bring my worst self to church.

And yet, there is this beautiful gap of time when I fall

to my knees and the body and blood of Christ, broken and spilled on my behalf, is offered to me. This is the gap between who I think I am and who Jesus knows me to be. Again, I am reminded: forgiveness, mercy, and blood spilled on the floor of my life, washing me white as snow. Christ sees my low anthropology, my sin, my mistakes and he allows himself to be hung, high on the cross.

His height meets my depth and the gap of grace saves me.

3

THE HOSPITALITY STING

If I had to pin down one law that rules my life it would likely be: Thou Shalt Be An Excellent Entertainer. As a Mississippian, I was raised to smile broadly at people I find tiresome and to entertain with the latest Junior League Cookbook. You know, life skills. Honestly, when I married a priest I was nearly as excited about the parties as I was about the Jesus. Suddenly, my domestic prowess could be put on display for the world to admire! How humble of me.

When I stumbled across a Bible study about hospitality, I immediately knew God had something *special* in store for me. I could use this study and really up my cocktail party game. Surely a few verses from the Good Book could make my pot roast more meaningful. As so often happens, God had other, less Sarah-as-hostess-with-the-mostess, plans.

As I do with every Bible study I embark upon, I obnoxiously told everyone I knew that I would be doing it. At church that Sunday I pulled one of my friends aside and showed her the study on my phone. "You should totally do it, too," I insisted. For the record, I had done exactly one day of the Bible study at that moment.

Only retrospectively am I able to admit that I wanted her to do it so that the next time she came for dinner, she would think something along the lines of, "Wow these gruyere canapés are great! And so HOLY." I needed her to think virtuously of me in all possible facets of my life. Because I long to believe that kind of nonsense about myself.

I have found in my spiritual life that themed Bible studies tend to double as cure-alls: Be a better wife, be a better mother, be a better hostess. It does not matter how much grace and forgiveness I hear; it is never enough. I invariably believe I am one "amazing" devotional away from spiritual enlightenment. So, per usual, I went skipping into FixMeVille. I was going to be the most holy and hospitable hostess this side of Mississippi. I would entertain the bejesus out of the masses.

Then, the unthinkable happened. I locked myself out of the house with a six-month-old baby in my arms. Our hidden key was nowhere to be found. My husband was hours away, on a lake, trying to catch fish. I called that friend who, just a day before, I had informed of my Best Life Now Hospitality Bible Study. She immediately dropped her actual life and came to my rescue. We drove to the school and picked up my hangry toddler. She bought me baby formula. We went back to her house and waited for my husband. It took him seven hours to get home.

When we got to her house, she immediately handed me a beer and began making plates of crackers and cheese for my family. In these days of "casual entertaining," one can easily fall into the trap of thinking that serving "rustic recipes" or using butcher paper/tea candles as my table decor is somehow less contrived (and therefore more blessed) than using fine china. It is not. It invokes just as much fear of judgment and anxiety. Real hospitality is opening your home as it is and offering whatever happens to be in the fridge. It is brave and vulnerable. It is crackers, cheese, and cold beer.

As the evening went on, she ordered pizza. She held my baby. She bathed my toddler. She gave me another beer. At some point, she handed me her phone to check a text message from my husband (because, of course, my phone had been locked in our house).

Maybe you can recall a moment in life when God shattered the Barbie Dreamhouse identity you'd built for yourself. When my friend handed me her phone, that's what happened to me. Staring back at me from the screen was the hospitality Bible study I had recommended to her only a day before. Luckily, it was just me and my baby in the room because I started openly weeping.

God didn't want me to undertake that study because he had some grand plans for me to become our Lord and Savior meets Martha Stewart. God intended for me to read the study because he wanted me to remember what it feels like to *receive* hospitality. Real hospitality. The kind where you sit on the floor chatting while your baby rolls around on a blanket. My friend had taken us in, fed us, and bathed us (my toddler, at least). It was Biblical. I was overcome with a kind of indescribable gratefulness.

Spirituality, especially women's spirituality, can be laden with self-improvement. There are an endless amount of "mores" in Christian woman blogs, books, and bench presses. We should love more, give more, be more hospitable. How can we change the world? How can we Proverbs 31 our way into virtue? How can we impress everyone who crosses the threshold of our front door?

But what if we've got it all wrong? What if our rightful inheritance is to be on the receiving end?

It is a risky assertion. There is an anxiety that if we saw ourselves as merely receivers, then we would not help the marginalized. We might forget the true widows and orphans in our midst.

The more I realize I need Jesus, the less I buy into that concern. As we hear hauntingly in 1 John: We love him because he first loved us. It is the reception of love that engenders gratitude. And gratitude does not a passive person make.

When Jesus tells us in Matthew 25:40, "Truly I tell you, whatever you did for one of the least of these brothers and sisters of mine, you did for me," he means everyone. All of us. As it turns out, there isn't even another line to stand in. We are all marked "The Least of These" in one way or another.

St. Flannery O'Connor wrote about just this very thing in her short story, "Revelation," where she writes the account of the insufferable Mrs. Turpin. She is an incredibly racist and classist character who doggedly believes she and her husband Claud are better than anyone else she knows. Sadly, all her self-affirming bravado makes her oblivious to the fact that she is an unbearable person.

But the Lord Jesus Christ will not let her live in this false reality any more than he would let me live in mine. Towards the end of the story Mrs. Turpin sees a vision. It appears to be a line of people marching their way into heaven. Only, nothing is the way Mrs. Turpin believes it should be:

> And bringing up the end of the procession was a tribe of people whom she recognized at once as those who, like herself and Claud, had always had a little of everything, and the given wit to use it right. She leaned forward to observe them closer. They were marching behind the others with great dignity, accountable as they had always been for good order and common sense and respectable behavior. They alone were on key. Yet she could see by their shocked and altered faces even their virtues were being burned away. She lowered her hands and gripped the rail of the hog pen, her eyes small but fixed unblinkingly on what lay ahead. In

a moment the vision faded but she remained where she was.

God was burning away the virtues these pious people had clung to. God was taking away every attribute Mrs. Turpin believed was of great importance. Flannery O'Connor understood that we are just like her godawful protagonist. We are all full of ourselves and therefore incredibly needy of God's grace. The goal of our Christian life has never been to make us better people. God does not desire for us to practice better hospitality or to claim to be more virtuous. In fact, God, in all his mercy, burns away those parts of us that we cling to.

It is the Parable of the Pharisee and the Tax Collector all over again (Luke 18:9-14). The Pharisee lobbed judgment and accomplishment up to God. "Look at my new napkins!" I imagine him saying, "I've got a wonderful recipe for something intimidating and French!" All the while the tax collector is standing there, locked out of his house in gym clothes, holding a baby: "Please help me, Lord. I need a friend and a beer."

My very virtues are being burned away. Thank God. I am being asked to give up on all of these ridiculous images I have of myself, and to face my self-affirming sin, so I can know God's gracious forgiveness.

Out of his sin and embarrassment, Scripture tells us, the tax collector offers the sincerest of prayers, "God have mercy on me, a sinner." He was the least, the last, and the lonely. He had no virtues of which he could boast. He knew he was always and forever on the receiving end of God's amazing grace. I am grateful to be in such good company.

4

THE PINK LETTER

As a kid, I was the unprepared daydreamer. Some of my earliest memories of school involve doing homework sheets on my morning bus ride. I forgot my book bag at home constantly. I never kept up with my lunch money. Early on, I remember thinking it was just a part of my charm. In elementary school, I had a teacher who decided it was her mission to cure me of my forgetful ways.

One day she was done with my nonsense. I cannot remember what I did to send her over the proverbial edge. But I definitely did something. She made a pink "O" out of construction paper and made me wear it all day long. When she taped it to my chest, she told the class it was okay to laugh at me. She wanted the O to remind me that I needed to be more *organized*.

That's right, people. I got a starter set for *The Scarlet Letter*. That night I sat in the bathtub and wept as I told my mom how embarrassing the day had been. My mother, who is the fiercest person I know save for her own mother, called the teacher at home. Whenever my mother is mad at someone, she will start talking to them by saying, "Here is what you are going to do." The next day my teacher pulled me out in the hallway and told me she was sorry. It helped. But the damage was done. I had been declared an unorganized mess in elementary school.

Some days, I feel like I should thank this teacher for diagnosing my absentmindedness early. She pushed a button in me marked "neurotically over-prepared" that I never could undo. I became a planner, a fastidious note taker, and the kind of person who is unable to sleep with dirty dishes in the sink. I may even have that teacher to thank for the very book that you are holding having ever been written. It takes a lot of organization to write a book. A whole pink O's worth.

Of course, she had pointed at the part of myself that I had the least amount of control over and said, "You need to fix this, little girl." I still grasp to control my impulses. I am desperate to always appear on top of things. Whenever people comment on how prepared I am for a meeting, I always think, "If you only knew how much I have worried over this very moment."

I also become anxious if I make a basic planning mistake. If I forget to sign a paper or get the time of a meeting wrong, I turn into a wreck. If someone innocently points it out to me, I have a hard time breathing. And if they point it out in front of other people, you will find me weeping inconsolably in the ladies' bathroom.

Email has proven to be my downfall. I know, it sounds silly. But I will spend twenty minutes rewriting a five-sentence email if it is going to anyone other than a close friend. I want to get every detail right.

Two particular examples stand out in my mind.

I share them because I know I am not alone in getting emails like these. I share them because I have sent this kind of emotionally shaming garbage to other people. I share them because we are all Broken Hearts with a Pink O taped to our chests. And I want you to know, even when the subject is painful—perhaps especially when it is painful—the grace of God is the only appropriate response.[3]

So there I was, minding my own beeswax, sending out an email to a group of mothers asking for money for a project that all of our kids were working on. I did not understand how the organization's funds worked. It turns out that when the email landed in everyone's inbox, one mother was having a terrible day. I mean, I do not know that *for sure*. But I hope she was having a terrible day.

She told me (and half a dozen other women that she had copied), this was not how the money worked. She wanted me to know I had gotten everything wrong. And she wondered how I could even be in this position with such little awareness of the details.

Her email brought back the sensation of standing in

---

3. With that in mind, the names and details of the Broken Hearts, both here and throughout the rest of the book, have been changed.

front of a room full of my peers with them pointing and laughing. It is a feeling I can always access, whether I want to or not. I felt as though all of my fellow mothers were staring at my email and thinking, "What an idiot. She's so unorganized. We should slap a Pink O on her."

I read the email in a parking lot. I sobbed quietly to myself for fifteen minutes. I wrote back a passive aggressive missive where I told her (and all those people she copied) perhaps I was not cut out for this venue of motherhood. I know, I am such a mature, self-actualized, Christian woman.

When I told some friends about the experience, they all seemed surprised it hit me so hard. To be honest, I was surprised too. I kept grappling with what this meant for me theologically. Am I not redeemed despite the words of my fellow mother? Am I not loved unceasingly by a God who forgives my every misstep?

Weeks later I got another email from another Broken Heart. This one had to do with my alleged inability to follow the rules. My son was taking some classes outside of school. I asked the person in charge about some of the protocol because I was genuinely curious. Not only was I informed that my question was ridiculous, I was told that "as a parent" I should know better than to ask it.

Needless to say, I forwarded this person's threat-level-ten email to several of my friends. Some of them suggested we start a girl gang and show the emailer who was boss.

While I appreciated their communal rage, I knew that my emotional response was as much Sarah-as-mother as it was Sarah-as-hurt-little-girl. I knew a righteously angry email in response never makes anyone feel better. Not for long, anyway. The only answer was Jesus.

So I did something I have never done before. I did not respond out of defensiveness or anxiety. I told the little girl with the Pink O taped to her shirt that she was beloved by God, and it was high time she acted on that incredible truth. In short, I responded out of the person Jesus says I am:

> Dear Brokenhearted Angry Person (kidding),
>
> There is no need for you to shame me about what I "should" know.
>
> I have plenty of parenting articles/advice/opinions out there that do that for me already.
>
> I am doing the best I can. And I am loved by a good and gracious God who knows that. Thank goodness.
>
> Go to hell (Still kidding. I said "Thanks"),
>
> Sarah

In response, I got back an apology and a reassurance that I was a good mom. Frankly, I had not expected this person to be so kind and generous in return. Email can make unintentional villains of us all. What struck me as odd was I did not *need* any follow up to what I had written. When

35

we clearly articulate our belonging to Jesus, it becomes more difficult for the world to get in a word edgewise.

It has become totally normal to spend five to ten years in therapy as a young adult. I certainly did my turn on the psychological merry-go-round. And I am all for everyone dealing with their pain and decades old wounds in a professional mental health setting. But I do not believe we will find a cure for what ails us in the office of a nice bespectacled man on the Upper West Side. I believe with every fiber of my being we must know who we are in Christ.

Everyone has wounds from childhood that will follow us into the grave. Christianity is not a magic potion to make our pain vanish. But it will tell you to whom you belong. That is the best way I can describe "putting on the armor of Christ" (Ephesians 6:11). We are not necessarily fighting a battle with other people so much as fighting our own well-developed patterns of self-loathing sin. We do not hate the people who send the emails quite as much as we despise ourselves receiving them. Jesus interrupts this destructive cycle. He puts a safeguard around our hearts and whispers, "Remember, you are mine."

Our despair is met with grace and forgiveness. While we may not be worthy of much on our own, through the cross we became worthy of God himself. Jesus came as a ransom for my unorganized, small schoolgirl self. He came as a savior for the deeply neurotic overworking mother I have become. He is the answer to the world's demands that we be constantly ashamed of ourselves. Jesus was with me when I stood in front of the classroom all those years ago. He was with me when I sobbed alone in that parking lot. And he was at my fingertips when I resisted the urge to email out of defensiveness and opted instead to email from the promise that Jesus is the very anchor for my soul (Hebrews 6:19).

For I am convinced that neither death nor life, neither angels nor principalities, neither the present nor the future, nor any powers, neither height nor depth, nor Pink Os taped to the chest of a little girl, nor chastising emails sent to the inbox of a grown woman, nor anything else in all creation, will be able to separate us from the love of God that is in Christ Jesus our Lord.

5

OUR BIG MOMENT

I once heard a story of a bishop who went to baptize inmates at a maximum security prison. Having never done this before, the bishop did not realize that he was expected to show up and work with whatever the prison provided for baptisms. So, instead of a quiet, small baptismal font, the prison provided him with a massive transparent tank of water.

A young man approached the tank. He had changed out of his orange jumpsuit and into a white robe. Up until that moment, the bishop had not realized that he would actually have to climb into the tank with the prisoner. In the Episcopal Church, we tend to baptize by sprinkling exactly three teaspoons of water over a gurgling infant's head. We do not, by tradition, climb into giant tanks of water with people who have been convicted of manslaughter.

The enthusiasm of the crowd reached a fever pitch.

The young man's fellow inmates were cheering him on as though he were about to do the world's most impressive keg stand. Of course, that is not what was about to happen. This young man was about to pin a name on what had always been true: that Jesus had died for him, too.

I was told that the young man exhibited a Babe Ruth level of confidence. At one point, he even raised his hands to the crowd: "Cheer me more!" Apparently, the bishop tried to nudge the young man gently towards the water. But his fellow prisoners would have none of that. They started yelling, "DUNK HIM." And so, the bishop did.

The thing about the story that has always stayed with me was not that the bishop was awkward, because being socially out of your depth in that situation seems pretty normal. What never leaves my brain is the description of the prisoner as he rose from the water. You would have expected him to barrel out of the water with some Rocky theme music playing. But that is not what happened.

Instead, the man stood there quietly, bent over. He looked relieved. There was no grandstanding, only a man who realized he had been redeemed, in a prison of all places. Jesus had happened *to* him.

So often our victory in Christ does not look like victory at all. It does not look like a grand moment where we are the center of the show. Most days, our life in Christ looks like the acceptance of defeat. Which is not exactly the sexiest of messages.

There is little to no room in American Christianity for

an understated experience. We all want a powerful testimony about how we came to Christ and everything in our lives changed. We stopped loathing ourselves. We became better parents. Our health improved. We want to feel as though we've made a bold choice to accept Jesus. We long for a glory story that gives us our big moment.

In the deeply religious culture of my high school, it sometimes felt as though everyone was falling off some Christian righteousness wagon on a regular basis solely for the thrill of dramatically climbing back on. One day you would make out with a guy from geometry class in the teacher's lounge, and that evening you would find yourself conveniently in front of a worship band, hands in the air, singing something about Jesus being awesome and *you* giving yourself to him. Again. As though Jesus needed to be reminded of his awesomeness and as if your new Christian goal-setting was going to get you anywhere.

I was never very good at hanging with these crowds. Partly, because I *liked* making out with nerdy guys in the teacher's lounge. Also, because I felt like Jesus already knew that about me and so re-re-rededicating myself to him in front of strobe lights and a fog machine was not going to help my case.

Only once did I attend a Bible study in high school. It was hosted by the local (giant) Southern Baptist church and was the only option for socializing one could find on a Wednesday night in Mississippi. I don't remember which passage we studied, but I do remember that the subject was about how we could *always do more for God*. This cattle call for Jesus begged an unanswerable question. I asked the leader how we could know if we loved God enough. I can still remember the desperate swelling of my heart as it longed to be sufficient for Jesus. Instead of offering me a word of consolation or compassion, instead of telling me that, as the old Methodist hymn goes, "Jesus Paid It All," she offered me more challenge in the form of a platitude. "Well," she paused, "just do your best!"

I remember thinking, "I don't even do my best for me. How in the world am I supposed to do that for God?" I remember feeling lonely and heartbroken. If my failed attempts to walk the moral high ground could not save me, then what could? If my moments of rededicating myself to God and promising that *I would do enough this time* kept failing, then what was the point of Jesus, anyway? I don't know in what emotional state I returned home that night, but my parents never encouraged me to go back.

When we come to Christ, it is because we are done doing our best. It is because we cannot even pull off our most mediocre. It is because we are done doing anything, ever, period, the end. It is because all of our magnificent moments have failed us, and we long for the sweet relief of Jesus.

The movement towards faith is less of a decision *we* make and more one that was made on our behalf, on a cross many, many years ago.

Some churches seem to position our conversion as a

kind of before-and-after photo à la *The Biggest Loser*. On the left, we see a sad, pudgy sinner and on the right, we see a smiling body builder for Jesus. I wish that was the way Jesus worked. But it is not. There are many days that believing in Jesus means I keep finding parts of myself that I despise. More sin, more brokenness, and more inadequacies make themselves known. So often the Gospel feels like I just keep holding up my broken heart to Jesus, waiting for him to tell me I have hit my forgiveness threshold.

"But you know *this* part about me too, Jesus? Right? Doesn't this make me ridiculous?"

"Yes," Jesus responds. "Even for that you are forgiven."

The longer I am a Christian, the more I find myself identifying with the sad, pudgy loser version of myself. Because the more I digest the fact that Jesus came to save me, the safer I feel in his love and the more I can see my sinful heart for what it is. I am broken and longing for relief. My relationship with Jesus does not make me feel like a baptized superhero. It makes me feel like a redeemed villain.

When our children were infants, we made the decision to start offering them communion as soon as they could eat a Cheerio. This was no small thing in our New York parish where many people came from Catholic upbringings. Most of them did not receive their first communion until elementary school. To be honest, I couldn't wait that long. I wanted our children to know that they belonged to God in a tangible way. They had been baptized and logically, for me, that meant they should receive communion. This was not about them having a big moment; it was about them knowing they had been loved and saved from the very beginning.

In seminary, I learned that Orthodox Christian traditions have no minimum age for receiving communion. The clergy can give an infant communion in the same service that the baby is baptized. Some churches use what amounts to a liturgical baby spoon to feed the newly baptized baby the body and blood of Christ.

This makes sense to me. Baptism is that moment when we say to Jesus, "I give up. I need your solace and forgiveness. I bring nothing to the table but my own broken heart." And that moment begins as soon as we acknowledge our belonging to him.

Perhaps we all want a Big Moment for our story because it makes us feel as though we get a say in how everything works. We want to tell the best parts of our story and leave all the horrible moments out. While our ego may tell us that *we* should be the ones to choose God, Jesus knows this is an impossible charge. As the Gospel of John spells out, "You did not choose me, but I chose you..." (15:16). God never charged us with the responsibility of saving ourselves, because he knew it would never work. And to believe otherwise is a paralyzing burden.

I suppose that is why the story of the baptized prisoner has stayed with me over the years. He came out of the water and saw the reality of his sin facing him in the form of orange jumpsuits, prison walls, and a nervous Episcopal bishop. Yet he knew that God had chosen him, loved him, and died for him. There was inarguable relief and forgiveness in that moment.

We are no different. We all rise from baptism and face the harsh realities of our lives and ourselves. We are astonished at the moment of crucifixion because it gives supreme love to murderers, bishops, and stay-at-home moms alike. We are astonished that God would love people who offer him nothing but surprised gratefulness in return. His love follows us and leads us, even when we are bound and determined to ignore him.

This quiet and unglamorous moment is where we find the truth. Our faith is secured, not in the stories we tell about ourselves, but in the person of Jesus Christ. His promise is not predicated on our puny millisecond of compliance, but in the three days on Calvary that saved us all. His immense moment of commitment—to us—happened long before we could ever think to commit to him.

6

A BRIEF ARGUMENT
IN FAVOR OF CHRISTIAN HYPOCRISY

If you want people to think you lead an amazingly pure Christian existence, find a stranger in the cereal aisle and tell them you are married to a member of the clergy. You will feel amazing afterwards. Trust me.

Cereal Aisle Stranger will make inexplicable assumptions about your righteousness. You and your husband pray together hourly. Your family memorizes a Bible verse every week.

If you let them go on long enough, Cereal Aisle Stranger will even glance at your children and comment on how "good it is" that they go to church every week because, "no one does that these days."

Of course, you and Cereal Aisle Stranger both know that this is not really about *you* but their own sense of what a *real* Christian looks like. We should embody their perfectly moralistic expectations, whatever end of the morality spectrum they happen to be working under.

I wish my family even remotely resembled their projection. The reality is, I will walk away from Cereal Aisle Stranger and immediately into the reality of my hypocritical Christian life. A life filled with gossip, self-loathing, and lines drawn in the sand of whatever desert I happen to be standing in. Best to deny their imaginary narrative and acknowledge the truth: clergy and their spouses are all hypocritical *because* they are Christians. And all Christians are perpetually saying one thing and doing another while wearing a cross necklace.

Avoiding so-called hypocritical Christians used to be a hobby of mine. In high school, I would walk by the Fellowship for Christian Athletes meetings on my way to my (less good-looking, way nerdier, and much less Jesus-y) International Thespian Society meetings. I would glance into the cafeteria full of football players and think to myself, "Those dudes look mean." I would go on to think how wonderful I was to be avoiding these large groups of Christians who bonded over touchdowns and Bible studies. I was far too serious and educated for that kind of nonsense. I was an elevated and enlightened Christian who *really got it*. Then, as now, I liked to think of myself as someone who walked the walk and talked the proverbial talk.

Unfortunately, I have not exactly outgrown my need to distinguish between myself and other, less righteous, believers. There is an entire market place out there for

Christian women who want to look more "Godly." We can get a chest-enhancing t-shirt with a quote from Colossians.[4] Or we can tote around ceramic mugs that read, "All I need is a little coffee and a lot of Jesus."[5] And then there is the issue of me telling strangers what my husband and I do for a living while standing in front of a row of Fruit Loops. I want to be clear that I am extra Jesus-y now. Do not get me confused with those other Christians who are ignoring our moral code of conduct.

Mostly, I think that Christians love to hate on the group marked "Hypocritical Jesus Jalopy," because we do not wish to be lumped in with their brokenness. We want to be the shiny new car that everyone notices. When the plain truth is that, while we may all crank, we're still rusty on the inside.

Our current political climate is constantly demanding that American Christians do what is right as defined by whoever happens to be holding the bullhorn. Jimmy Carter, Bono, and the Russia-peering porch-gazing Sarah Palin, among others, wish to define for us what ethical Christian behavior looks like. As much as I want to join their proud world-changing brigade of hymn-singing, I find myself incredibly grateful that Carter, Bono, and Palin are not actually Jesus. They do not get to say who is in or who is out. Which is good news, because on their terms, and on the terms of humanity in general, I would

---

4. Have it.
5. Want it.

always be in the "discard" pile.

No matter what your political stance is on global poverty or how many times you have used an expletive in the past week, it is on this collective helplessness that we hang our hats. What makes us Christian is that we desperately need Jesus.

There are no hypocritical Christians. There are just Christians; the hypocritical aspect is a given. When we read St. Paul's assessment of his own faith in Romans 7, "I do not understand what I do. For what I want to do, I do not do. But what I hate, I do," what we are reading is a concise statement on what it means to be an authentically neurotic Christian aware of his or her own hypocrisy. We are powerless over ourselves.

At times, I can be baffled by the dichotomy that is allowed to exist in the average Christian's character. I desperately want everyone to pick a lane and stay in it: You either believe in Jesus and get your life together, or you can be someone fun who I could hang out with on the weekends.

Christianity happens in the valley between these two swamps. Our faith occupies that wasteland in between the sinful shadow of our present selves and the shadow of the Cross where our future selves reside. The death of Christ on the cross is the proof text that binds us together. It is in this valley that we surrender our broken hearts to Jesus.

We are hypocrites day in and day out. We do the thing that we hate to do. Our salvation is absurdly unfair.

We are ridiculous sinners whom God has chosen to love through the person of Jesus Christ. In church we loudly sing the hymn, "They Will Know We are Christians by Our Love." Good Lord, I hope so. But in the meantime, they will know we are Christians by our hypocritical sinfulness and the Rescuer who pulls us from this wretched estate.[6]

Perhaps the best way to respond to Christian hypocrisy is to laugh at it. Because it is so painfully true. People have been calling Christians hypocrites forever. And that is because we are. We screw up and Jesus loves us anyway. That is crazy talk.

6. Many thanks to Sally Lloyd-Jones, who calls Jesus "Rescuer" in her incredible *Jesus Storybook Bible*.

7

THE WORK OF LOVE

Our son Neil was born a sleeper. He could slumber through an ambulance siren. We once took him to a traditional Passover Seder that was hours long—and loud. Our rabbi friend commented that he had never seen a baby sleep so soundly. I told him Neil had always been that way. To which he replied, "You should keep that to yourself. No one likes a show-off."

We had no idea how lucky we were. I just assumed our next child would be equally easy to please. But our daughter Annie was the opposite, and it hit me like freight train. Around the time of her first birthday, people remarked to me repeatedly that they could not believe a year had gone by so quickly. Often, I had to hold myself back from yelling, "It took forever! I remember all of it! She was awake the entire time!" She did the classic newborn every-half-hour-wakeup-call and then proceeded to withhold a solid night of sleep until she was thirteen months old. Yes, I know you might have some advice for me about how I could have handled this better. But she sleeps now. So, it's too late.

Annie's disinterest in sleep was the first time I wanted my small children to hurry up with their childhoods. I remember being at a Whole Foods during the great Sleepless Troubles and noticing a middle-aged couple sitting together at one of those tables, having a glass of wine. Meanwhile, I smelled like breastmilk and body odor. My shirt had a mysterious stain on it. Watching this well-rested couple laugh together made me realize that I've yet to reach the level of chicness required to drink alcohol at the grocery store. Obviously, I wanted to kill them.

I longed for the day when we would not watch the sunrise while giving our baby girl a bottle. I missed the fact that I used to get up and go to the gym. I just wanted to sleep.

And then, due to nothing but biology and her decisive will, Annie began to sleep through the night. It was a minor miracle. For a few weeks, I enjoyed it. But soon, part of me missed the midnight feedings. I missed that tiny baby. It dawned on me that giving up chaos might also mean giving up tenderness.

Our daughter had demanded so much from us. Her restlessness meant that every time we went to her in the middle of the night, we were called to love her in deeper and more intentional ways. Over the course of that year, we saw little Annie at her most needy. We were tasked with comforting her and being gentle with her. We had no idea the gift we had been given.

Annie stretched us as a married couple in many ways. Someone had to get out of bed in the middle of the night. Someone had to make the bottle. Someone had to give it to her. Often, one of us would head to the kitchen and the other would head upstairs to the rocking chair. It was a midnight ballet.

Marriages without children are by no means incomplete. But, my goodness, do babies make your devotion to one another precise. We did not realize that we were engaging fully in the work of love and that we would miss it when we no longer leapt out of bed together at our child's behest.

These days the patterns of our life are somewhat easier. Annie is two, and our son Neil is five. They can play together, and no one needs a nightcap bottle anymore. There are still the daily tasks of being a parent: loading and unloading the dishwasher, folding an endless mountain of laundry, and making yet another peanut butter and jelly sandwich. We get more sleep, but we are still tired. I have learned to nap through an episode of *Curious George* like it is my job. I continue to have moments when I wish that these intense years would just fly by.

It is at night that I feel the pang of my children growing up too quickly. Often, I pick up toys right before bed. And I'll see these little vignettes of precious items that my children have put together. Annie will have positioned a princess in one of her brother's Lego creations. Neil will have found a way to tie all his stuffed animals together so he can "wear" them.

Before bed, I will head upstairs to check in on how they are sleeping. I almost always find that my son has decided to change out of his pajamas and into his Halloween giraffe costume. Once he found a permanent black marker and drew stick figures all over his legs and face. He looked like he had just gotten out of prison. If I am longing to touch one of them, I will ease our daughter out of her crib and rock her for a few minutes. It is strange to only be a year from her babyhood but already nostalgic for what once was. I am in disbelief at how quirky and sweet they are. And I cannot believe that they have been put into my care.

One day very soon this will all be different. In ten years, we will have kitchen cabinets that are not scratched. In another ten years, our laundry will fit into one basket. Part of me longs for this future point in time. I want to be the gray-haired couple that shares a glass of Willamette Valley Pinot Noir while deciding what they should pick up for dinner. It will be so pleasant to go home to a calm house with only a small dog to greet us. Everything will be incredibly clean.

And yet, within the chaos comes so much tenderness. When I think of my favorite moments of the day right now, they are filled with effort and love. Each evening, when I get our daughter ready for the bathtub, I lean around her, my body cradling hers with both of us standing, and I take her diaper off. She always pushes out her round little tummy for me to pat it. When I place her in the water, I must convince her that the black things floating in the tub are not bugs but the dirt she brought in. Then I get on my knees, and I wash her with soap that smells like vanilla and oranges.

Honestly, I have a difficult time believing that anything in life will be more beautiful than that moment.

Whenever I am around older women, they always tell me stories about these moments with their own children. And I cannot help but marvel at a God who gives us enough energy to do the work of love and makes our hearts tender enough to miss it.

In recent years, there has been groundbreaking work around the treatment of Alzheimer's patients and how to navigate their memory loss. In previous generations, it was believed that you should remind them of what they are forgetting. You should make them try to think of what year it is or correct them when they call you the wrong name.

Thankfully, much of this is changing. Now, we are told to "play along" with people who are losing their precious memories. If a patient believes they are twenty-three years old, when they are actually eighty-three, we should ask them what it feels like to be so young. Clinicians have noticed that elderly women with memory issues are often elated to be given a baby doll. They will hold the doll, wrap it in blankets, and sing to it, just as they did their own babies decades before.

When my own grandmother faced dementia, she moved into a retirement community that could help her better navigate day-to-day life. My grandmother was a farmer's wife who raised three children in rural Mississippi. Her background was similar to that of the women on her hallway. They were elderly ladies who had been wives and mothers as young women. They took care of children during the day and brought lunches to their husbands out in cotton fields.

When my son was born, we tried to go and see her as much as we could. I have a lot of happy memories from those years. Once, my mother brought in a little plastic riding tractor for our then toddler-aged son to play with while we visited. It was hot that day, so we stripped him down to a diaper and let him barrel up and down the hallway on the toy. As I walked down the corridor with him I noticed that all these elderly women had come to their doors to watch him with expressions of joy on their faces. He reminded them of something that happened long ago, but still felt so fresh and tangible decades later.

After Stephen Colbert's mother died in 2013, he dedicated a segment of his television show to her memory. Colbert said of her:

> In her last days, my mother occasionally became confused. And to try to ground her we

would ask simple questions like "What's your favorite color?" or "What's your favorite song?" and she couldn't answer these. But when asked what her favorite prayer was she immediately recited a child's prayer in German that she used to say to my eldest brothers and sisters at bedtime when they were living in Munich in the late 1940s. Her favorite memory of prayer was a young mother tucking in her children. We were the light of her life and she let us know it until the end.

It is hard to recognize that you are in the sweetest time of your life when you are in it. People often say to young parents that "the days are long, but the years are short." They are right. In a very short time my children will be adolescents, and then teenagers, and then I will have one very quiet house. I know that there are happy years beyond these. But for some holy reason, these are the years we return to in our memories, even decades later. I am convinced that the work of love we do stays with us no matter how much time has passed.

8

BRING YOUR BABY TO HOSPICE DAY

Parents today are raising a bunch of ice monsters. At least, that's what the endless stream of articles explaining how to "teach" compassion seems to suggest. We are told to talk to our kids at eye level or to let them speak at great length about their feelings. We worry that we must train them to be emotionally reflective human beings. Because raising a sociopath would reflect poorly on our parenting skills.

I'm sure this stuff works. But I have other advice. If you want your kids to be empathetic, let them watch a lot of *I Love Lucy* and encourage them to overeat at social gatherings. Incidentally, these two things may go hand in hand.

In our ninth grade year, my very best friend Emily suddenly lost her father. He died one night of a heart attack. She lived five houses down from me. There were summers I saw her family more than my own. When her daddy died, she was sadder than anybody I had ever met.

This was the January after the movie *Titanic* was released. Radio stations were playing Celine Dion's "My Heart Will Go On" as though they were playing it especially for Emily. She was not fun to be around. She cried randomly. And there seemed to be no end in sight. Yet opting out of being her friend was not something my parents would have allowed. I don't remember much about the days that followed, but I clearly remember my parents kept sending me down to her house. I would try to come home and they would say, "Oh, just stay a little longer." We had another friend named Clint whose parents apparently did the same thing.

A few days after the news hit, Emily's house was filled with people. Clint and I were sitting on the couch where her dad had died. We had a bowl of M&M's and one of us dropped the whole thing in the couch cushions. We started laughing hysterically. Immediately, we got a glare from the local soccer coach but, given our proclivity for high school theatre, neither of us cared. Other people started to laugh. We even got Emily to chuckle a bit. It occurred to me, this is what we could do for her. We would eat funeral food, overstay our welcome, and not freak out when she cried.

This is basically everything I needed to know about being a priest. In my first job in ordained ministry, I served as a hospital chaplain on what people ominously called "the Liver Floor." This wasn't a job the more seasoned chaplains wanted. Probably because, to be quite honest, alcoholics are mean and they smell bad. And the Liver Floor was full of them. I quickly learned that if I walked into a room and there was a skinny elderly man in bed watching anything with John Wayne in it, I was about to get yelled at. Initially, this made doing visits fairly difficult. But like the persistent teenager who eats all your banana pudding and encourages you to cry when Celine Dion croons about lost love, I was determined that these guys would let me hang out with them.

I kept going back, knocking on their doors, cup of coffee in hand and talk-yelling, "Hey! I'm the chaplain! What's the Duke up to now?"

Eventually, my relentlessness wore them down. Most of them were lonely and scared. Being on the liver transplant list as an alcoholic is a tall order. You must complete a rehabilitation program, submit to random drug testing, and attend Alcoholics Anonymous meetings with regularity. Those were the easy rooms. Sometimes, I met people who had checked all those boxes and then fallen off the proverbial wagon. Those were uncomfortable, often hopeless rooms. Fortunately, I had learned years ago that my job was never to keep people from suffering but to just sit there with them as it happened. My childhood experience taught me to overstay my welcome. And so that is exactly what I did.

People often wonder how to respond when their friends' lives are in crisis. In ministry, I am often asked,

"What do I say to someone who has just lost their father, or their baby, or a friend?" You say, "I'm sorry, this is terrible," and then you hang out for a long time. You may be thinking, "But what if I hang out too long? What if they want me to leave?" Well, you being annoying has given them something else to focus on. You should feel good about that.

Honestly, if we want our kids to be empathetic, we should just throw them in the deep end of the suffering pool. All too often we sign our kids up for community service projects or mission trips hoping this will somehow engender a sense of compassion. And then we shield them when our neighbor's husband dies. We do not want them to see the kind of pain that they themselves might experience. We do not want our children to be faced day after day with that same mourning widow. The problem with our ambitious save-the-world-ism is that no one learns empathy by being benevolent. We learn empathy by letting our ninth grade friend cry into a pizza.

In his classic book *Kingdom, Grace, Judgment*, Robert Farrar Capon tells the story of the Good Samaritan in the most insulting way possible.[7] Most of us read this parable and like to identify with the Samaritan himself. We like being the hero. But Capon says we are wrong. He

7. Capon also bravely included in his assessment, "This means, incidentally, that Good Samaritan Hospitals have been otherwise misnamed. It is the suffering, dying patients in such institutions who look most like Jesus in his redeeming work" (323).

writes that if there is any imitating of Jesus to be done here, it is that Jesus saw himself in the poor and the sick and the outcast. Jesus, Capon boldly asserts, is the guy left for dead on the side of the road. In other words, it is not in some self-aggrandizing act of service that we see ourselves as being Christ-like; it is in remembering that other people are beloved. And that we are beloved. And that there is no difference between us. This is the clearest path to empathy.

We learn empathy by witnessing people in the midst of their pain and by walking the uncomfortable road with them. Age wise, empathy can start early. My mother inadvertently encouraged me in this parenting model when our son was born. Whenever I would tell her about a funeral or a tough hospice visit my husband had to make, she would say, "You should bring the baby. Babies are so oblivious, and people love them."

We heeded her advice. I hauled that kid to nursing homes and the bedsides of the dying. And what happened was always miraculous. When you are flat on your back waiting to die, everyone looks sad to see you. But not babies. They are clueless. Babies see you and they are like: Hey! A New Person! I LOVE YOU!

I've often wondered why hospices don't have a Baby Visiting Program the way they bring Yellow Labs around to lie in bed with the sick and dying. Babies are the best. They don't see illness or fear; they toot and giggle and like to be held.

These days, I don't haul my five-year-old and two-year-old around the hospital with me. Nor do I tell them a lot of stories from my job. I have come to realize that it is not just the "very important work" I do that teaches them to empathize. Instead, it has been noticing the moments when people have taken in our family and loved us unconditionally.

Not so long ago, we had one of those weeks when it felt like the whole house was falling apart—body, mind, and spirit. Our shower poured water into our first floor, I got into a car accident, and we had to send our elderly dog home to Jesus (or wherever). The people who stepped in to help were people who knew us well. They knew that we love to entertain, and so the water coming out of our ceiling was high drama for our Southern sensibilities. They knew that car accidents are terrifying for anyone, but especially for my skittish self. They knew our tenderhearted kindergartener would be a mess for weeks over the loss of the family dog, so some of them showed up to console him more than anyone else.

Comfort food rolled in immediately. Roasted chicken, macaroni and cheese, brownies. A delivery man showed up with warm cookies and milk. Somebody brought cherries and watermelon. The house filled with peonies and roses. I could hardly look around without feeling grateful and weepy.

And then there were the offers to just hang out with us. A more reasonable line of thought made me want to turn these friends down. Did I need people to come and play dolls with my daughter? Was it necessary for my son to have companionship while he watched a Netflix movie? Well, no. But empathy, real empathy, looks like the unnecessary.

Empathy is a poor use of time and resources. It is not gallant and spiritualized. Empathy is eating too much food and overstaying your welcome. It is watching Nicholas Sparks movies and crying until you dry heave together. It is re-enacting that skit from *I Love Lucy* where you shove chocolates into your mouth. Because it makes you laugh. And it makes them laugh. And you love whoever "them" happens to be.

9

I SEE DEAD PEOPLE: WHY HOSPITAL CHAPLAINCY IS THE GREATEST JOB EVER

For an off-hours hospital chaplain, there's no more awkward question than "What do you do for a living?" Mostly because telling people that you hang out all day with the sick and the dying makes you sound like a much better person than you actually are.

During my stint in hospital ministry, people would often gush, "Gosh, I don't know how you do that. I could never do that. That's amazing." To which I would often respond, "You could totally do what I do, it's not that hard." After all, they often had much more difficult jobs than mine. School teachers, hair stylists, farmers—those are real and often thankless jobs.

Hospital chaplaincy may not be hard, but it *is* rewarding. You walk into a room where people are lonely and scared. Your only job is to listen. That's pretty much it.

And you get to eat the nurses' donuts and, depending on the hospital policy, wear a white lab coat that you have clearly not earned. It has everything I look for in a profession: conversation, fried food, and a spiffy outfit.

In most jobs, there is very little room for error. Teachers cannot give their students bad information if they want them to pass the test, and hair stylists would lose their chairs if they gave everyone Rihanna's latest shaven coif. But hospital chaplains can kind of bumble around, uttering a solid 70/30 ratio of stupid-to-wise things, and people still think they are remarkable.

Of course, I know why everyone believes that hospital chaplains constitute an army of angels. We hold the hands of the brokenhearted, the lost, and the lonely. It is not unheard of to meet people one day and watch them die the next. And while that makes us sound like the most selfless saints on the planet, such highfalutin notions are total bullhockey. The real secret is, what makes chaplaincy the greatest job on the planet is that you regularly witness death.

Death used to be something everyone saw on a regular basis. It was a normal part of being a human being, because we mostly died at home. A few generations back, it was typical to put your dead relative's body on display in what was called the "parlor" of your home. There, with your shiny knickknacks and sitting couch, you would have old Aunt Myrtle propped up for everyone to pay their funerary respects. Imagine, real dead people in your house.

And it's not a horror movie.

Remarkably, this began to change with the Civil War. In order to get soldiers' bodies back to their families, they had to be embalmed. Up to that point, embalming was a fairly uncommon practice, but the deluge of casualties made it into a popular profession almost overnight. These newly minted morticians soon realized that not everyone wanted to have a dead body on display in the front room of their house, that they could make money centralizing the whole process. Thus the parlor room we once had in our homes became the freestanding funeral parlors that we all use today.

And in a transition that speaks to just how ready we are to deny death, we began calling those front parlors in our homes the "living room." BECAUSE WE WILL LIVE FOREVER.

For the first time in the history of humanity, many of us can live a life where our death might be the first death we see up close. We can die "neatly" in a hospital room with as much or as little family contact as our relationships demand. The cost of this is great: Death is no longer a part of life. Instead, it has become a devastating impossibility that always happens.

As a chaplain, part of my responsibilities was to pray with families in the moments leading up to the death of a loved one. Chaplains almost always get called when patients are taken off of life support. In the movies, this is a very quick process. The patient gets unplugged, and his or her heart stops. In real life, these things take time. People can survive for hours or even days after they have been removed from the machines. There was usually time to chat with the family, or sit in silence and listen as the patient's breath began to slow. I would often stand around the room for a while, asking questions about the person in the bed and praying for his or her family.

The first time I attended a death, I was sent to shadow one of our more seasoned chaplains, a guy named Steve. We got the call that a woman had suddenly suffered a devastating heart attack. Her family wanted chaplains to be present as they made the decision whether to pull her off of life support. We gathered in a side room far away from her dying body. I was so relieved. Steve was incredibly pastoral with the family. He listened to them wonder their "what ifs" aloud, and he hugged them while they wailed. I just sat there in stunned silence. Finally, they made the decision to let her die that afternoon. Steve and I were free to go back to the office. I remember wondering if it was too early for a margarita.

As I headed toward the elevator, Steve headed back to the hospital rooms. "Where are you going?" I asked him. "Her family isn't even in the room with her."

Steve smiled. He knew I was new and dumb and scared. He gently prodded me, "We need to go see her, too, even if she doesn't know we are there."

I put my head down and begrudgingly followed my afternoon mentor down the hallway. He walked into her room and got as close to her soon-to-be dead body as he could. He put his head against hers and whispered, "Sweetie, I am so sorry this has happened to you. You are so loved. And you get to go home to Jesus today." Steve had never met this woman. I am almost certain she did not hear him.[8] But he knew something that I would have to learn. Being a chaplain means that we get to be with people at the most important moment of their lives. You show up when they die. It is a privilege and a lesson each time.

Some months later, I was on call for the first time, and my pager led me to the room of a woman I had never met before. She had been dying of cancer for months. When I arrived at her bedside, I was met by her four adult children and her very elderly husband.

There was no room we could slip away to so that I could avoid witnessing the extent of her sickness. I had no wise words to offer a family who had seen such significant suffering. In fact, the longer I stood there, the more unnecessary I felt. But I had learned from Steve that you just stay there and listen. Maybe, even if you are of no use, you will learn something.

As I stood in the room with this family, it became obvious that the only relationship that mattered was the one between the husband and his dying wife. Everyone else

---

8. I would later learn that hearing is the last sense to go before we die. Apparently, it is always worth whispering love into the ears of the dying.

was just a well-meaning third wheel. I would learn that it was often like this with the elderly couples. So much had existed between them. Years before their middle-aged children were born, these two people had met and fallen in love. They had survived years of joy and heartache with one another. They had stories we would never know. Who really knew the secrets and experiences that knit them together?

There I was, fresh out of seminary, on my first solo death call, totally unsure of what to do. I mumbled through some prayers and offered a listening ear. I cannot honestly say that I presented anything helpful.

But here is what I remember: No one could convince the elderly husband to sit down. As his wife slowly died, he bent uncomfortably over the bed with his arms cradling her vulnerable body. He was determined to stay fixed that way. We were all worried he would pass out. I kept trying to encourage him to sit. His adult children would push chairs behind him, saying "Take a seat, Dad. You can just hold Mom's hand." Finally, he hushed us all and insisted, "She always loved it when I held her. So I'm going to hold her now."

The romance of when they first met, the wedding, the first baby, the second, the third, and the fourth, the fights about who would unload the dishwasher, the worry about how they would pay for college, the joys (and fears) of being empty nesters, the devastating cancer diagnosis, his steadfastness, her pain...this is what their story had boiled down to. And he did not want to miss a moment of it.

I was given a small glimpse into the kind of sacrificial love that God gives us when we stand in front of one another as younger, naiver, skinnier versions of our current selves and covenant with one another "till death do us part."

That experience was an incredible gift to me. I remind myself when I hold my husband's hand that there will be a last time for us to touch, a last time to worry about college loans, a last time to fuss about domestic chores. I remember that the most selfless marriage is the best marriage. I recall that suffering alongside one another is much better than suffering alone.

At this point, I have prayed for hundreds of couples in hospital rooms. I have seen a tremendous amount of death. And it has taught me the greatest lesson: We all die. And I do not write that as some kind of a dark and sad reminder. And I do not mean it as some sort of a seize-the-day mantra. But instead, as an encouragement.

When we remember how temporal this life is, we can find true consolation there. Our inadequacies, concerns, failures, and self-justifications will all go peacefully home to Jesus. In Revelations 7, we are told that God will wipe away every tear. I think it is safe to assume he will also wipe away our inadequacies, concerns, failures, and self-justifications. Seeing death has made me live in the hope of going home to Jesus.

Retrospectively, I was not smart enough or compassionate enough to be a hospital chaplain. No one really is. Instead, I was lucky enough to get a front row seat to the tremendous love and loss that is the fate of everyone.

10

HOW DATING A JEWISH GUY PREPARED ME TO BE A PRIEST'S WIFE

When I was a freshman in college, I fell madly in love with a Jewish guy I had known for years. He had been much more popular than I was in high school, so when he decided I was cool enough to date in college, I felt like I had won the relationship lottery. We dated for almost three years. In Mississippi's unwritten rules of courtship, we were bound for marriage.

This is the part when I'm supposed to tell you my deep regret at not having dated a nice Methodist Sigma Nu at Ole Miss. This is where I'm supposed to tell you that my time spent dating a Jewish guy was my "wandering in the desert." Perhaps you're expecting me to confess that no matter how much I repent for that era in my life, I continue to feel guilty for being such an unfaithful sinner.

To quote the internet, LOL. God is more complicated than our black-and-white moralistic narratives long for him to be. I learned more about what it means to be religious and in a relationship in those three years of dating than I ever did from any of those terrible college Bible studies I attended.

Pretty much everyone in my life was supportive of our relationship and where it was headed, save for my Mississippi Memaw, who assured me that College Boyfriend would eventually know Jesus. I, on the other hand, was sure it was going to be less of him getting to know Jesus and more of me working on my guttural pronunciation of "Baruch atah Adonai" for our Shabbat dinners.

For a while, I tried to be okay with this. But there were moments when I knew things were unraveling. Once, very early in the relationship, he purchased a child's workbook for learning Hebrew and we spent an entire plane ride going through it together. I remember being so moved by his kindness and one hundred percent freaked out by my reality. But I had become good at squashing that second wave of emotion.

One evening, in my senior year of college, I was sitting in synagogue on a Friday night, and the least opportune thing happened: Jesus decided it was time to intervene. I was sitting there singing the prayers, minding my own business, when I heard from a few pews back, "Sarah, honey, this isn't your place. It is time to come home." I did not turn around. I did not respond. But I knew it was Jesus, and I knew he was right.

We never know what God has planned in our lives.

Now, we say this kind of thing all the time, but what we really mean is, "I know what God has planned. He has *my* plans planned." Of course, this is never the case. God's plans are not our plans. God's ways are not our ways.

Case in point, dating a Jewish guy inadvertently prepared me for being a priest's wife. Stay with me.

Soon after we started dating, I dove head first into trying to learn everything I could about Judaism. I learned how to make challah and say very basic Hebrew prayers. I read loads of books about conversion. For a year, I drove up to Memphis from Oxford, Mississippi, to attend Friday night Shabbat services—when I love, I love hard.

When College Boyfriend became president of his university's Hillel House, I knew I had my work cut out for me. That year, for the Israeli Independence Day Party, I pulled out the traditional American flag cake recipe my family made for the Fourth of July. Only, I left out the strawberries and made a giant Star of David out of blueberries and Cool Whip. The partygoers were wowed. The cake was fun and joyful. It was my crowning Charlotte York Goldenblatt moment.

I realize this sounds trite, but entertaining is one of my favorite things about being clergy. And not because I am particularly good at polished silver and cloth napkins. We have done fancy Christmas dinners and run out of eggnog. Once, when we hosted the matriarch and patriarch of a parish, I burned the hell out of some nice steaks. When Hurricane Sandy hit New York, we ran a do-your-laundry here-is-some-soup camp out of our rectory, because we were one of the only houses with electricity. I'm not the world's best entertainer, but I learned many years ago that joy and fun are all anybody wants anyway. And if you can make an Israeli Flag with dairy-free whipped topping, then all the better.

Of course, the obvious thing that happened in those years of dating a Jewish guy was that I learned to talk openly about religion. College Boyfriend and I talked about religion because we *had* to. So much of who we were and what we believed needed to be hashed out. And while this is certainly not unique to interfaith couples, none of my roommates seemed to spend much time with their significant others parsing kugel recipes or explaining Easter mimosas.

Whenever I meet couples who tell me they "have not decided about religion"—and it's more often than you'd think—I am dumbfounded. The institution of marriage is so beautifully and deeply connected to religion. Also, marriage is jarringly difficult. You will fight a lot, you will yell at one another, and you may even fantasize about smothering your beloved with a pillow. Tenets like grace and forgiveness are crucial for a marriage to survive. So, take all the religious help you can get. Sort out the religion card with the person you are going to spend the rest of your life trying to love. Figure out if you want a Christmas tree, a menorah, or one of those creepy elves. And then pick a lane.

When my husband and I started dating, I was unafraid to tell him what I expected in the religion department. I was open about my questions and the answers I needed. Had I not dated someone of a different faith, I would have been hesitant to talk about my belief in Jesus. But when you've gotten as close as I had to telling Jesus, "Thanks but no thanks," you become a lot more open about how much he means to you.

Finally, and on a related note, dating a Jewish guy taught me how to sit in a pew by myself. And I am forever grateful our Lord saw fit to give me a preview party. College Boyfriend only came to church with me a handful of times. It was never going to be his thing. So, when I wanted to go to church, I went by myself. Towards the end of our relationship, I remember watching a father lead his son up to the communion rail. It wrecked me. I thought, "I must marry a man who can lead our children up to receive the bread and wine." And I was devastated by the idea that my worship life would consist of me sitting alone in a pew.

Then I married a priest. And I am almost always in a pew without him. And he is almost always on the other side of the rail. On the rare occasion that we are on vacation and my husband does bring our children up to receive communion, it is never the bucolic picture I have in my mind. It is often an awkward and hilarious experience. Because, you know, Josh is never actually *with* us in worship.

So guess who still didn't end up with a Mr. Rogers-type who would hold her hand during worship? Guess who got a family that fails to look like a Normal Rockwell painting at the communion rail? This girl. I see what you did there, God. And I like it.

I look back at that time in my life and wish I could tell young Anxious College Sarah that it was all going to be fine. I wish I could tell her the religion thing would undo her first real love, but it would not be her undoing. Had you told nineteen-year-old me I would have ended up married to an Episcopal priest, I would have asked you to pass me what you were smoking. Because it must be good stuff.

People love to say, "Man plans and God laughs." Perhaps. I think it is more likely we plan and the Lord redeems whatever plot we have concocted for ourselves. I marvel at what God was doing when he had me date a nice Jewish guy for those three sweet years. He was teaching me what it felt like to fall deeply in love. I learned how to host a houseful of people with confidence. I became unapologetic in my devotion to Jesus. And yes, God wanted me to know that I could spend Sundays in a pew, sans husband, for the indefinite future.

Sarah plans and God prepares her for something even more beautiful. Thank God Sarah is not in charge.

11

SAVED BY JESUS (AND THERAPY)

When I was in college I had a very painful falling out with one of my oldest friends. It was public, and I was mean. Even though I wanted to move on with my life and never talk to her again, I could not shake the incident. I had been awful to her and no matter how many times I told myself that I was "right," I could not believe my own story.

This was the era of Jewish College Boyfriend. I told him that I simply did not know how to handle this situation. He told me that his synagogue was on the verge of the High Holy Days and that it might be the perfect moment to seek my friend's forgiveness. I had no idea that Judaism encouraged this kind of person-to-person repentance. During the High Holy Days, Jews observe the Ten Days of Repentance where certain prayers are offered, charity is suggested, and repentance is demanded. Much like Alcoholics Anonymous espouses in its infamous ninth step, Judaism beckons the repentant to seek the forgiveness of those they have hurt.

I wrote my friend a letter. I don't remember exactly what I said, except that it felt as much like the truth as I was capable of telling. I said that I had been hurtful and mean, and I asked for her to forgive me. I told her the honest version of my story. I felt crappy and needed her to say she forgave me. And, graciously, she did. I remember being struck that it took an entirely different religion to make it possible for me to say that I was sorry. It was the first time I felt like I was being honest about who I was, even if it meant me owning up to my worst parts.

This was a part of a general sea of change that took place in my twenties. I started what would be a decade of therapy and eventually had what I can only call a gospel conversion. My version of Christianity had always been about doing good to make up for the bad. In other words, with enough good works, I could make my story sound better. As I grew into adulthood, I began to realize that I was just lying to myself.

I had to be honest about who I was in Christ if I wanted any real sense of peace in my life. I needed to be real about the fact that my story was the story of a sinner. I was not a victoriously moral individual. I had no righteous wisdom to share. Like the Samaritan woman at the well (John 4:1-26), I needed Jesus to say, "I see you. I see your sin. And I'm here to save you."

One of the more challenging rituals of seminary usually took place during the first few weeks of school. We would be asked to go around the room and to tell our story. This was intended to be a lovely exercise where everyone felt heard and understood. But given my human nature for pooping in Paradise, I saw it as the perfect moment to talk about how incredibly interesting I was.

I had "facts" about my life that I would always share. I lived in New York (which meant I was important), but I was originally from Mississippi (so, folksy with an accent). I was married to an Episcopal priest (so I knew more than all of you naïve fools combined). While I felt guilty for glossing over a lifetime of bad choices and hardship, I knew that I needed to look like the shiniest chalice in the cupboard. And so, I headed straight for the sin of omission.

The odd thing about seminary is that you get to know your classmates quite well. I once heard the seminary environment described as being like a cruise ship. You get up in the morning and pray with a group of people, you eat breakfast with them, attend class with them, head back to church with them, have dinner with them, drink with them, and, depending on your marital status, you may even sleep with them that night.

So, this yearly telling of our stories began to take a new shape for me. These people knew me, like *really* knew me. They knew I struggled with not feeling smart enough. They knew I was either in the throes of morning sickness or spending sleepless nights with a newborn. Some of my good friends even knew if I had yelled at my husband that morning before class.

As I took my place at the octagon-shaped table every year to share my story, I began to let go of my need to curate it into something it was not. I started to tell my actual story, the one about my sin and Christ's redemption. The one where I remind myself of all that God has brought me through, despite my profound lack of trust. I began to tell people that I feared motherhood and that being married to a priest was much harder than I ever expected it to be. I told them I almost left Christianity completely.

After our first two years of seminary, I noticed that we all became more honest about who we were. I began to wonder if our professors asked us to do this every year, not because they needed a refresher on who we were, but because they needed us to give up on dancing our well-dressed skeletons around the room. They needed us to tell our actual stories for our own sake. We had to drop the I-am-so-amazing monologues in lieu of whispering our truths to Jesus at the well.

Several years ago, there was a fun cultural moment where people were asked to write their own "Six Word Memoir." I remember hearing about it on the radio and immediately the phrase, "Was saved by Jesus and therapy" popped into my mind. I had not had time to think about something witty and poignant. I was alone in my car, so the performance aspect was gone. It continues to be the most honest version of my story that I have.

We live in a culture where "telling your story" is practiced and celebrated. While I like the sound of that level of sharing, I require the subtext of the cross to give my story its real rhythm: sin, sorrow, redemption, gratitude, sin, sorrow, redemption, gratitude, and so on. If left to my own devices, I will tell the story about myself that makes me the most likable. I will try to be charming and funny. I will want desperately to look like the most professional and religious seminarian (or mother or wife or priest) in the room. Nothing I say will be true, and I will become exhausted by the sound of my own voice. As much as I need honesty, I need Jesus to keep me honest about who I am.

We worship a God who finds us at the well and tells us all about the life that we thought we had kept hidden. We are loved by a God who offers us living water so healing, we cannot help but drink it. Even after a history of self-destruction, meanness, and denial, Jesus meets us at our point of greatest need and promises blanket forgiveness. Even after a day of profound self-justification and self-serving lies, we fall into bed at night and hear Jesus tell us, "I know you. And I love you, still."

I need the context of Someone Else for me to truly

be myself. I need the safety net of the cross in order for my story to be honestly told. I need reassurance that this bleak and beautiful planet is not my soul's final resting place, and my sins are not the final word. If I am going to tell my story, and tell it true, then I need Jesus to be my merciful narrator.

12

FAMILY SECRETS ARE MY FAVORITE

In my final year of seminary, we had a speaker come talk to us about something (allegedly) important. But all I can remember him saying was that young people did not care about their ancestry. He told a story about watching *The Prince of Egypt* with his young son. In case you are not hip to DreamWorks Biblical classics, *Prince* details the life of Moses and, as such, contains quite a bit about Moses' lineage. The speaker's son picked up on that element and asked his father a very simple question about his great grandfather. It turned out that not only did he not know the answer to his son's question, but he realized he did not actually care.

He went on to explain to us that people do not care who their great-great-aunt was. Or what their ancestors did to make money. Or how many children their grandmother chose to have and why. He claimed our past histories were uninteresting to this generation we call millennials.

I get it. The world does not function like it used to. Family just doesn't mean as much as it did a generation ago. We do not need our grandmothers to watch our children while we tend the fields, because our grandmothers are going to their morning Zumba class and our kids are getting dropped off at expensive daycares. Very expensive daycares. We do not *need* to know our family the way we once did.

And yet, I am not sure I can get on board with the assertion that our family and its history is of little consequence to our lives.

As a wide-eyed twenty-eight-year-old entering seminary, I quickly surmised there were two kinds of people in my classes: those whose grandmothers went to college at eighteen years of age and those whose grandmothers did not. I fell into the latter category. But I had always felt that my grandmothers (and frankly their grandmothers) had everything to do with me getting a graduate level education. My maternal grandmother went to cosmetology school and became a hairdresser in her thirties after the death of her first husband. My paternal grandmother went to college in her forties after she too became a widow. She became a special education teacher in the Mississippi Delta. Their stories made my story possible. I see the hand of God in their struggles and accomplishments. I cannot imagine not knowing about them, and I am slightly (okay, sinfully) judgmental of anyone who does not care.

Worse than ignoring our family histories, it felt like

our speaker was dangerously close to telling a room full of students that we were all there on our own volition— as though our intentions for our lives somehow mattered more than our God-given history. His assertion made me wonder exactly how he thought he had been given the opportunity to speak to a room full of students at a highly regarded university. I wondered how he justified his own existence. Did he simply wake up that morning, call in sick to McDonald's, and decide today would be the day he would become a professional speaker? Of course not. People, perhaps generations of people, had all brought him into this moment. And there he was, unknowingly pissing me off.

When word got around in my family that after enduring sixteen years of Mississippi public school education, I would be attending an Ivy League seminary, my father sent me a one-line email that read simply:

"This means so much for our family."

So, as that ~~idiot speaker~~ beloved child of God stood at the front of lecture hall and told us all he could not answer basic questions about his family and *isn't he so coy and modern*, all I could think was, "Would that I *could* forget those who came before me." Would that I could.

Of course, he was simply reflecting the zeitgeist. We are constantly being told to throw off whatever family we came from in lieu of whatever Brand New You we would like to curate. Naturally, anything interesting about our family lineage should be lost in the wash.

The problem with our devil-may-care approach to ge-nealogy is that life does not work that way. We cannot throw off Grandmother Ethel or good old Uncle Enoch (real people in my family) so easily. Often in Scripture study we come to those lengthy passages where so-and-so begat such-and-such. Our tendency is to skip over these parts because it is hard to imagine that they matter. But undeniably, they do.

They tell us generations of people sacrificed and loved their way into the next generation. They tell us we did not just hatch from an egg and follow a pathway marked "Success." When we take our history seriously, we gain invaluable perspective. In looking at one branch of names after another, we find that the most important thing we do in our lives may simply be to just live them.

What a relief! We are not the shining star of our fam-ily tree. Instead, we are one of many beloved children of the Father. Our lineages are written onto the heart of God, because they tell the story of his ongoing faithful-ness and love.

When I found out that our second child was going to be a girl, I was elated. I screamed into the phone when the doctor told me her gender. I also remember being imme-diately struck with the weight of what we should name her. Many women begin planning their future daughter's names as third graders, and I was no exception. When I was in high school theatre, I was a big fan of "Scarlet Juliet." In college, my propensity for Southern literature propelled me towards combinations like "Flannery Eudora." Our daughter was very lucky to have been born *after* my flair for naming children after personal hobbies.

Still, my husband and I found ourselves a bit dumbfounded when we learned that God had given us a baby girl. Could we agree on a name? As luck (also known as God's providence) would have it, my mother and I had begun some long neglected ancestral research. My grandmother had recently died, and it felt like we could finally dig in some corners everyone had previously agreed to ignore.

It took very little digging to discover that our family's claim to be humble, Louisianan white folks was untrue. Somewhere in my great-grandmother's generation the decision was made to hide that fact that our family has been Spanish for as far back as we can trace. At this point, it is safe to say that our lineage would be considered culturally Mexican. We come from a little town in Louisiana called Zwolle, and my basic knowledge of the place is people know it as a "Mexican" town—and have for many generations. We, somehow, convinced each other we were the only white folks from around there. This is sad, bizarre, and hilarious. At least to my modern sensibilities.

This discovery shed some serious light on things. It explains my grandmother's, my mother's, and now my inexplicable affinity for obnoxiously Southwestern décor. It explains some of the food we eat. It even explains the need to hold our family reunion at a place the old folks called

"Sammy Gill Park." Years later we would come to realize that the area was in fact called San Miguel Park. Seriously, we always called it Sammy Gill.

My family's remarkable history had been hidden in our names. For generations, my female ancestors bore names like Candelaria, Maria, and Polita. In a single generation those names became Ethel, Emma, and Betty. Not to be overlooked, there was the Ygnacia del Rio who would later be known as simply "Nancy Rivers." Obviously, this sort of discovery leads to more questions than answers.

It would have certainly been *easier* to have had Anglicized names and hidden the traditional ones. But we will never know why this major part of our family identity was swept into the tamale masa, and I wanted desperately to bring it into the open. When it came to naming our daughter, we knew we wanted to choose a name from this previously concealed line. Blessedly, a name my husband and I had always loved was staring at us from right there in my Latino family tree, "Anastacia." It means "resurrection," and since our daughter was to be born in the season of Easter, it felt like God had placed her beautiful name right in our laps.

I'm probably putting undue weight on a baby name. But I wanted to give her something that speaks to her past. I wanted her (and our family) to understand that God made her incredible family line with Anastacia Joy Condon placed purposefully in the year 2014, and generations of beautiful, proud people had led to this moment of her becoming her.

Our collective histories tell us more about our present selves than we could know on our own. We learn that we did not bootstrap our way onto the planet. We were intended to be here. So often we speak of ourselves as being a part of the family of God, but we forget we are just one generation in two millennia of believers. The people that came before us had names, and prayers, and a deep belief in Jesus Christ. They left us churches and traditions and promises that the Gospel would be proclaimed, no matter what.

Ultimately, of course, we have all been grafted onto the lineage of Christ. When we read in Ephesians 1:5 that God adopted us to be his children through Jesus Christ, we should take comfort in our place as beloved sons and daughters. And we would be foolish not to take a gander at his family tree. Our Lord and Savior hails from a prostitute, an adulterer, and a thief—and those are just the types of sinners that got written down. If you follow the list all the way to the end, I believe you will find your name there as well.

13

THE DEAFENING LEGALISM OF SWIMSUIT SEASON

I have concluded that if a thirty-something suburban mother is interested in remembering what it felt like to be in eighth grade, she need only visit her neighborhood pool. There, you will find several mothers standing around in the shallow end with their large sunglasses, wide brimmed hats, and body image issues galore.

One evening, I was at our neighborhood pool for (ironically) "Burger Night" when one such mother joined our shallow end awkward party. She was, easily, the hottest one of us. As she waded in, I noticed she was holding a smoothie in her hand.

> Mom in a Lands' End Swim Dress: Is that a SMOOTHIE?
>
> Hot Mom: Yes. I can't eat burgers anymore. I've got a fat roll coming in.

There are two normal responses that we women are supposed to have when our skinnier and better looking friends tell us they are overweight and hideous.

A) We can hate them and tell them so.

B) We can exclaim: "You're not fat! You're so skinny! I'm fat."

Normally I would have chosen one of those options, but I just didn't have it in me. I wanted to hate her. I really did. I wanted to revert back to eighth grade and call her some horrible name (behind her back—we are talking about eighth grade), and never speak to her again. She was a babe! How could she stand there among her soft-around-the-middle peers and telling us *she* had a fat roll?

For one glorious summer of my life I looked great in a swimsuit. I was eighteen, eating mostly sugar-free jello and running like there was a fat monster chasing me. After that season of inexplicable joy, I began to loathe wearing swimsuits as much as the next American woman.

Two things happened that changed my disdain for the pool. First, we moved to Texas where swimsuits are the yoga pants of suburbia. Which is to say, everyone wears them all the time. Then I had a daughter and read a bunch articles suggesting the best way to keep her from being overly body-conscious (also known as having her own "season of jello diet") was to actually wear a swimsuit around her. I determined to change my swimming-pool-avoiding ways. Not only was I going to get a swimsuit, I was going to get a bikini. That's right. Slow metabolism and stretch marks be damned, I was going whole hog.

I headed to my local department store and tried on like three hundred swimsuits. It was in a mostly empty, overly-lit dressing room. And it was the loudest my head has been in years. The voices that spoke to me came from all over the spectrum.

First, there were the usual suspects. The voices fixated on issues like cellulite, love handles, and the aforementioned stretch marks. I battered myself around a bit for putting on fifty pounds (I know, I know) with each of my pregnancies. But then I remembered how good all those hamburgers and milkshakes were, and thought, "Whatever."

Then there were the voices of feminist rhetoric I've been hearing for as long as I have been on the planet. They told me to embrace my body and love my curves. Because that *always* works. Alas, while I long to be the Gloria Steinem of swimwear, I simply cannot. My body is still my body. I do not look in the mirror and feel some level of sexual empowerment. I look in the mirror and see a somewhat out of shape mother of two children.

Finally, the Summer Modesty Police popped in to my brain. They are the worst. The SMP tells women we should cover our midriffs, especially once we've become mothers. Perhaps if this had been more engrained in me as a child, I would be better about keeping it all under a Lilly Pulitzer cover-up. But I am first and foremost someone who loves efficiency and comfort. I've got three words for the Gospel of the One Piece: it is hot. And by that, I mean temperature-wise. I am not about to cover that much—sorry I'm not sorry.

All of this is to say, I stood in front of the mirror and realized I had no idea what *I* thought of the swimsuits. Which is crazy-making. I could only conjure images of Heidi Klum and feel inadequate. It was so loud in that quiet dressing room not even Katy Perry singing "Roar" over the department store speakers—you can't make this stuff up—could make me feel better. I quite literally could not hear myself think.

Finally, I yelled aloud to no one in particular, "Stop telling me what to do!"

This was the moment it hit me: What I look like in a swimsuit does not matter. And it never will. I did not come to this conclusion because I have some grand mantra I whisper to myself every time I wade into the matriarchy shallow end. The way I figure it, if I am very lucky, I have another fifty summers left in me. Another ten where my kids will still want to play in the pool with me. Another two where I'll be holding a baby in the shallow end. I realized in the dressing room of a Kohl's department store that this was likely the last summer that our schedule would allow us to go to the pool almost every day, just as the sun was setting.

In the sixth chapter of Matthew, Jesus boldly advises, "Therefore I tell you, do not worry about your life, what you will eat or drink or about your body, what you will wear. Is life not more than food and the body more than clothes?"

When the hottest Mom at the pool showed up on Burger Night with a smoothie in her hand, all I could think of was how hard it can be to hear Jesus above the noise. It can feel impossible to hear Jesus when he tells us not to worry about what we will eat and drink and wear. Some days I just want to write off that long-ago, Middle Eastern rabbi as a guy who just doesn't understand how difficult his commands can be.

These days, telling people not to worry is a part of the zeitgeist. It is one of those overused pop psychology phrases we throw around like, "Choose Joy!" or "Be more vulnerable!" Well, sure. That sounds great. But choose joy how exactly? And be vulnerable to whom? I find joy in the fact that Jesus has given me unmerited grace. Call me limited, but I cannot be truly vulnerable to anyone but Christ himself. If you are going to tell me not to worry, I need to know why. Because simply telling me to not worry is asking me to give up something very near and dear to my tan lines. When Jesus tells us not to worry in Scripture, I believe he is doing something very different from popular culture. He is not telling us what do to. He is telling us who we are.

Too often we read those words of Christ and the Commandments from God and we feel the burden of behavior. Too often we believe that God is "telling us what to do" because he longs for some sort of a moral or feminist (or morally feminist) society. But this is not what God wants. God looks to a suburban pool full of body-worrying women and says over us, "Do not worry," because he longs for us to remember we are his daughters, and we are beloved.

God himself knows the brevity of this life he has given us. We know not the day nor the time of our death. The last thing our blessed Creator would want us to do is to waste a moment of our lives agonizing over a polka dot bikini. His edict for humanity to "not worry" is because God, through Jesus Christ, wants goodness and mercy for us, not worrisome weariness.

When we remember how treasured we are by God, the shallow end of the pool begins to look very different. The anxiety which comes with donning swimwear around strangers lessens. If the hot mom happens to blurt out her smoothie theology, we listen, and then we ask her if she takes her burger well done. Because life is so short, and we are loved so very much.

14

THE CHURCH IS STILL AWKWARD
ABOUT LADY PRIESTS

A long time ago, in a diocese far, far away, I was taking a major test for ordination. On the second day of the test, I had a first trimester miscarriage. I was lucky in that we were not far enough along in the pregnancy for the baby to have to be surgically removed. I was unlucky in that this meant for the next few days I would be "passing" the fetal tissue on my own. When I called the powers that be and explained to them that my having a miscarriage in the middle of a major test might be challenging, I was told I needed to "just push through it." I actually laughed-cried when I got the news. Sure! I'll *push* through a miscarriage for the sake of an ordination exam! No problem! And so, I proceeded with the exam for the next two days all while being an emotional and physical mess in a public women's restroom.

The experience would serve as an early signal to me. I would go on to be told my maternity leave "wasn't necessarily guaranteed." I would be told that weeks after giving birth I would be expected to work a half-time/no-pay job. I would be told it was entirely inappropriate that I was not behind the altar on Sunday mornings. And I would be told all of this by people who thought of themselves as feminists and supporters of women's ordination.

I laugh, heartily, when people suggest to me that my church, the Episcopal Church, is accepting and welcoming of women's ordination. Honestly, the more you tell me you are gung-ho about my being ordained, the more I look for the nearest exit. The most challenging situations I have faced as an ordained woman have been times when things were so "politically correct" and "liberal" that my gender was completely distorted. Instead of asking the church to name the discomfort and newness of ordained women, we just start trying to shove women into a man-shaped box. And y'all know good and damned well we are going to take up more room.

When clergy girlfriends call me to ask for advice about accepting a certain position or interviewing at a church, I have begun to say, "Ask them what they think about motherhood." Because if they do not love it, if they do not treasure it the way you do, then run screaming in the other direction. The church, in its newly empowered women's wisdom, believes that the best way to support us is to pretend like we are weirdly superhuman. And I'm over it.

There is an entire segment of the church that believes it supports us because we are interesting maternal oddities. This is not helpful. They believe we are spiritual superheroes who can celebrate the Eucharist and make babies. We can be real mothers and mothers in ministry! We can wear a stole one moment and a nursing cover the next! How novel! While I appreciate the enthusiasm, it fails to grasp the reality of my circumstances. I am not a feminist art installation. I am a mom who is a priest. It is really not that exciting.

Then, there is that massive part of the church which has all sorts of plans for us. Too bad we keep getting in the way! We have children, we have husbands, we refuse to overwork. This ambition-driven part of the church wants the ladies to be in charge more. It would be great if we could have a quick maternity leave and show up seven weeks later looking like we didn't just push a small watermelon out of our nether regions. You are most welcome for that visual.

Of course, a lot of the issues young clergywomen face go way past child bearing.

Right after I was ordained, it was suggested me that I dress more "calmly." When I asked for a further articulation of what my ontological apparel goals should be, I was told "more business, but not quite a Hillary Clinton pantsuit." To which I replied, "I feel like you should try saying that to me again in a different way. Because I think what you just said might be illegal. And I'm fairly certain cropped purple pants aren't going to hurt anyone."

One would hope that while navigating such uncharted territory, a girl could lean on those women a generation or two older. The problem is that I seldom, if ever, feel as though I meet their requirements. I have been in rooms where older women have looked to me to answer for my generation's shortcomings. They tell me the church is not what they thought it should or could be, and that my generation of clergywomen have been apathetic or "worried about the wrong things." I feel as though I'm navigating a landmine of middle-aged aunts who seek only to direct their ire at me. Only, I'm too busy changing diapers to give a what-for.

Part of me—the gracious part—understands their frustration. They had a vision for what they thought feminine power should look like in ecclesial and political arenas. From their vantage point, my generation has fallen short.

But the Real Sarah is like, "How about y'all start asking why childcare for clergy events is such a chore for every diocese I have ever encountered? Do you know how short our maternity leave is nowadays? Has it occurred to you that I may never want to refer to God by the feminine pronoun?"

I want to be very clear: I am grateful for the women who have come before me, politically and religiously. I was raised to be a feminist. But the brand of feminism I was raised with meant I was able to have choices the previous generations of women did not have. Feminism has never meant previous generations of women now get to name my reality for me.

Honestly, there *are* some late night phone calls with peers where we just sigh to one another and say, "This is bleak. And lonely." But I was not ordained into whatever the most exciting programmatic version of ministry would save the church. I was ordained to be a minister of the Gospel of Jesus Christ. I cling to that reality and try to ignore all the rest.

I find it's more comfortable to name how strange and relatively new it is that someone like me would be charged with the duties of administering the Word and Sacrament. In church culture, things had been clicking along with only men running the show for a very long time. It has been forty years since the first woman was ordained in the Episcopal Church. Based on my rough timeline, the church is about to be premenopausal on the subject of lady leadership. To act as though everyone should be on board and completely understand our vocation is shortsighted and ludicrous.

Ultimately, when the church and her members are not sure what to make of us, it isn't personal. At least, not necessarily. As in all relationships, grace, forgiveness, and a tremendous amount of humility are the best way to answer a community coming to terms with itself. For better or for worse, ordained women must navigate this world with prayer and honesty.

We are the ones being told our colorful cropped Ann Taylor pants are not "work appropriate." We are the ones who have more politically correct titles than an actual minority group (Mother Sarah? Sister Sarah? Rev. Sarah? Sarah Sarah?). We are the ones who have been asked to push through a miscarriage for the sake of a stupid test. It is up to us to tell our story. But let us heed the sin that lives in our hearts and be very careful how we tell it.

First and foremost, we are not walking "teachable moments." It pains me to hear my fellow clergywomen trying to justify themselves to people unfamiliar with ordained women. As a hospital chaplain, I quickly learned that nothing broke down relationships faster than me "educated-lady-'splaining" to patients why they sent a woman to minister to them. Instead, a simple, "They started hiring women! I know. Right?" followed quickly by, "How are you feeling? Can I pray for you?" typically shifted the conversation to what mattered.

Similarly, we do not need to apologize for the calling that has been placed on our lives. All too often, I hear some clergywoman say that she got ordained, but she just doesn't know how she "feels about it." Here's my suggestion: Feel good about it, and find something else to think about. I know it's not always that simple, but if we believe in a sovereign God, then he has placed us in this very moment to do this very ministry. God cannot use us if we are consumed with our own self-narrative about being *amazing* any more than he can use us if we are consumed with *how we feel* about us.

We do not need the validation of the entire planet.

We do not need a stamp of approval from anyone but the Triune God. And that already happened. God called us into ministry. The Holy Spirit empowered a bishop to ordain us. And Jesus spoke a word of worthiness over us. Which means, as my grandmother would say, we do not need to explain nothing to nobody.

As ordained ministers of the Gospel, we have been trusted to share the news that Christ Jesus came into the world to save sinners. Our place of honor is found at the bedside of the dying. We are entrusted with placing bread into the hands of the sinsick and whispering to them, "the Body of Christ, the bread of heaven." Pulpits stand in front of congregations for us to preach forgiveness to the broken-hearted. How humbling. How incredible. It is ridiculous that anyone could be called to such absurdly beautiful work.

Ordained women are not here to be a good story. We are not here to serve some political agenda in the church. We are here solely to serve the Gospel. The rest is just noise.

15

I AM THE PATRIARCHY

Some years ago, I was an exhausted new mother, unshowered, lucky to have made it out of the house with a child in tow, sitting in a Bible study with women who looked just like me. In a confessing moment, one of my fellow mothers blurted out, "I text my husband terrible things late in the afternoon."

We all nodded, knowing exactly what she meant.

"You know, it's the end of the day," she continued. "I have the kids on my own. And I'm just done. I'm waiting for him to come home. I start sending him these really angry messages, like 'When the hell are you coming home?' or 'OMG, WHEN THE HELL ARE YOU COMING HOME?' One day he says to me, 'Babe, could you send me nicer texts in the afternoon?'" We all laughed in solidarity. I started sending angry, overwhelmed mother texts just weeks after we had our first child.

Motherhood has its place of valor and admiration.

Whether we work outside or inside the home, there is a continuous stream of voices telling women we matter and our efforts are important. There are countless blogs encouraging mothers to be vulnerable, feeling creatures.

The same has not been true for men. The pressures men experience have yet to become a sincere conversation, at least not in the same way. The men I know simply do what is expected of them. They get up in the morning, work all day, come home, try to connect emotionally with their children and spouse, work more, go to bed late, and then do it all over again.

I am married to a guy who is a professional leader. He puts in long days, runs big meetings, and attempts to do his very best. Meanwhile, I bring in *some* income with writing and part-time ministry work, put food in a crockpot, spend an incredible amount of time with my children, and talk on the phone to my mom, a lot. His work makes my life possible. Period. The end.

I wish I could keep all of this in mind when he comes in from a fourteen-hour day at the office. But I am mostly incapable of that. Instead, when he confesses exhaustion or says to me, "I don't know if I can keep up this pace," my anxiety goes sky high. I want only to offer the directive, "You better. I really like our house."

It wasn't until Brené Brown's *Daring Greatly* made its way onto my nightstand that I began to look at the men in my life in a different way. I'm referring primarily to my husband, father, and son. In one anecdote, she explained everything to me. Brown describes signing books after a lecture she gave on shame. She was approached by a husband and wife. When the wife walked away, the husband lingered to chat. He asked her about her research on men and shame to which she replied, "I haven't done many interviews with men. I just study women." To which he replied, "Well, that's convenient." He went on to say,

> We have shame. Deep shame. But when we reach out and share our stories, we get the emotional shit beat out of us... My wife and daughters—the ones you signed all of those books for—they'd rather see me die on top of my white horse than watch me fall off. You say you want us to be vulnerable and real, but c'mon. You can't stand it. It makes you sick to see us like that (84-85).

Brown goes on to describe the research on shame that she began to do with men. It is staggering. When she asked men to talk about what shame means in their lives, words like "defective," "weakness," and "soft" came up. Men, she found, see shame *itself* as failure. Meaning, a cycle of "failure to shame to failure to shame" must be a very common experience for many men, particularly those in leadership positions.

What is it like to feel defective in masculinity? What must it be like to come home to a household that demands you *just keep going*? What is it like to get a text from your wife at 5PM, after a day of masculine performancism, demanding you get home *immediately?* What is it that drives men at such an alarming state? Brown's most indoctrinating research came after she began to study men more intentionally:

> I was not prepared to hear over and over from men how the women—the mother, sisters, girlfriends, wives—in their lives are constantly criticizing them for not being open and vulnerable and intimate, all the while they are standing in front of that cramped wizard closet where their men are huddled inside, adjusting the curtain and making sure no one sees in and no one gets out. There was a moment when I was driving home from an interview with a small group of men and thought, Holy shit. I am the patriarchy (95).

I read that paragraph one night and literally said aloud, "Holy shit, I am the patriarchy." I heartily recommend it as a confession for any angry texts you might have sent. As controversial as it may sound, we need men to keep functioning as they always have, neurotically and without question. We do not want to hear about their feelings. In fact, it would be convenient if they just did not have them.

We need the men in our lives to keep up with demand. They need to believe that they can do all things through their testosterone that strengthens them. Frighteningly, men actually tell themselves they are superhuman, just to keep it together. Statistically speaking, men believe they are smarter than they are. Men will apply for jobs when they meet only 60% of the qualifications. They are *four times* more likely to ask for raises than women. Faulty feminism has often told women that we should emulate our gender counterparts in their anxiety-driven craziness. But rather than copy it, I think most women just hope men continue to keep up this insane mirage.

What does all this mean when it comes to raising a son? What does it mean for a wife? How should we look at the men in our lives, grown and not?

On one of those hottest of all Texas days, I found myself standing in a parking lot attempting to get our infant daughter into her car seat while our three-year-old son ran amuck around the vehicle. An elderly couple walked by us, and the husband laughingly remarked, "Well, he's all boy, isn't he?"

Instead of affirming the commenting stranger, I said, "Well, we are still hoping he's a little Broadway, too!" It is best not to bother mothers loading their children into hot cars. You may not get the answer you were hoping for.

I glanced at our son. He was trying to climb through the trunk of our car while making truck noises. He did, admittedly, look very much like a little boy. And I wish I could keep him that way forever. Because I know what awaits him in the years to come.

Honestly, I have no idea how to prepare Neil Francis Condon to be a man in this burdensome world. Nothing short of everything will be expected of him: attentive to his family and devoted to his job, incredibly successful while making it look easy, and all the while keeping his own feelings and emotions in check. I worry and wonder what fatherhood and marriage will look like for him. Will even more be expected of our all-boy?

In good moments, I remind myself I am steering more of the ship than I care to admit. I remind myself that each time I chastise my husband for not being enough, our son watches and learns that men are, perhaps, never enough. I pause and remember the Gospel promise that we are all enough in Jesus.

The words of Brené Brown haunt me. Women are not the only ones who carry a burden of trouble and shame. But so much of the time, it feels like we are the only ones allowed to admit it. Men were not made to hold up the world by themselves.

Life and identity are infinitely more complicated than we want them to be. Our fathers were not made to be hardened statues of strength. Our husbands are unable to walk this world in denial of their vulnerability, allowing us to fall apart while they keep themselves together.

Our sons, God willing, need to know this consolation is true: The men in our lives need saving. The dads out there need a Father. They need the Prince of Peace, who meets us in our self-doubt. Our Good Shepherd, who sees our hidden pain. The Lamb of God, who takes the weight of the world on his shoulders and exchanges it for his uncompromising grace.

16

WHOLE FOODS CLOSES AND THE WORLD FALLS APART

Last year something very horrible happened in the life of our five-year-old son. After months of anticipation and suburban rumor, we learned that our Whole Foods would be moving across the street.

Initially, this life-altering event seemed like good news. Our favorite over-priced grocery store was suddenly going to have even more space to sell us organic bison probiotics. They would carry the shiny accoutrements that came along with a new building. Best of all, they were moving right next to that sacred chapel of motherhood, Target. Suddenly I would be able to purchase affordable curtain rods and organic cheese sticks in a single stop. By all accounts, my quality of life was taking a meteoric rise.

The news hit our five-year-old like the family pet had just died. When I exclaimed to him, "Neil, we are getting a new Whole Foods!" he immediately burst into tears. "But, what about our old Whole Foods?" he wept and yelled, "WHAT WILL HAPPEN TO IT?" That is, hands down, the hardest I have ever worked to not laugh at our child's tear filled face. Since I am not a total monster, I looked at him and said with feigned enthusiasm and comfort, "It's okay, buddy! I'm sure it will be fine!" To which our son demanded, "I have to say goodbye to the old Whole Foods. OKAY?!"

Thus began the Condon family saga called "When does our small child get to say goodbye to the old Whole Foods?" For a few weeks, we completely stopped eating organic vegetables because I could not face making the trip. I did not have it in me to let my young son have a therapeutic moment in a grocery store. Thankfully, my husband did the deed. One day, when we really "needed" local chicken breasts and fresh mozzarella, Josh hauled both children to what we now had to call "Old Whole Foods" and told Neil in the parking lot as they were leaving, "Alright buddy, this is it. Say goodbye to Old Whole Foods." And he did. Josh told me it was a teary, brief, and apparently necessary adieu to an old friend.

I marvel at these moments with our children. What we expect to be sentimental to them often is not. And when we believe a life change will be of little consequence to them, they have the unique ability to show us there is a different way to view the world. When I can step out of my adult pragmatism, I see where our son is coming from. Grocery stores are places we go to more often than we go to church. They are filled with snacks and bright lights. And, at Whole Foods, kids get to push around a tiny shopping cart and beg for cupcake samples. Sacred ground was shifting under his feet.

Months later, our ground would be shaken in a way that none of us were prepared for. On the morning of May 29th, 2016, there was a shooting in our neighborhood. It was identical to what we keep seeing in our news cycle. A random, mentally ill man with a high-powered weapon showed up on our streets and started trying to kill people. Friends called and told me to take the kids inside. We have doors with huge windows, and I knew I needed to block them. I made a game out of telling the kids to stay low to the ground and kept silently praying that no bullets would make it to our house. Neighbors a street over texted to say they had heard gunfire. Our two-year-old was blissfully oblivious to everything happening outside. Unfortunately, our five-year-old was not. There were helicopters overhead for hours, and Neil sat dutifully on the couch alerting me each time one flew over. He was so scared. He just kept asking me, "Why does someone want to kill us?" over and over again.

Weeks later my husband and I were in the kitchen having an unrelated conversation that, looking back, should have waited until after the children were in bed. Yet we proceeded to talk—paying no attention to the fact that Neil was hanging on our every word. We had been hearing news about globally persecuted Christians and were remarking about how sad and difficult it must be.

Finally, our son looked at me and said, "Mama, why are those people being killed?" To which I replied, "Because they are Christians." Neil took a moment and sighed with great relief, "Gosh, I am so glad we aren't Christians."

I immediately turned into a televangelist. "OF COURSE WE ARE CHRISTIANS! We believe in Jesus! You have been baptized!" I yelled back at him.

I was having my own specific moment of self-justification and mighty righteousness. How could my Pharisee-Level Church-Attending child not understand that he was a Christian? Where had we gone wrong? I was ignoring many of our day-to-day interactions in that moment. Neil knows who Jesus is and what happened to him on the cross. He can tell you about the conversion of Paul or the resurrection of Lazarus. But in his little brain, believing in Jesus had not attached itself to the title of "Christian."

Frankly, I was—and still am—taken aback at how shocked Neil was to find out that he belonged to a Christian family. Neil looked like he had been betrayed. "We are Christian?!" he said with terror in his face. "All of us?"

While I wanted to correct his misstep, I noticed how pained his face was. Neil had just been through a shooting, an event of real life terror right in his neighborhood. The last thing he needed was something else in his life that made him feel unsafe. The last thing he needed was for the world to feel more inexplicably sinful.

As a young, childless laywoman at my first church in New York City, I volunteered to teach Sunday School to elementary-aged children. I was terrible at it. Every week I would prepare a lesson that ended with powerful wisdom like "Be nice" or "Listen to your parents." Instead of talking about Jesus, I was life-coaching them for ethical behavior. To be fair, most of my content came from an actual Sunday School curriculum. Even the alleged church experts think it is our role to make children "better" people.

It would take years of life and the Gospel of Grace for me to realize what a poor excuse for a Sunday School teacher I had been. Children are not here for us to bend them towards our moral will. In fact, they are not here for *us* at all. Children *are* us, three-to-eight decades ago, before we became so bewildered by the realities of this world that we simply stopped looking at them.

We often count on children to be the court jesters of our lives. They say adorable things and have no idea how funny they are. They freely pass gas without apology. Yet, these are actual human beings. And they are coming to see the world as it really is. Which is an exacting and terrifying experience. How must it feel to be so moved by a cute stuffed animal that your eyes get a little teary? What is it like to believe that gummy bears are the height of culinary development? What must it be like to watch helicopters circling your house, looking for a man who is shooting at your neighbors?

All of this makes me wonder what exactly we are supposed to glean from the book of Isaiah's oft-quoted verse about the role of children:

> The wolf shall dwell with the lamb,
>
> And the leopard shall lie down with the young goat,
>
> And the calf and the lion and the fattened calf together;
>
> And a little child shall lead them (11:6).

We are mistaken if we believe that this passage has anything to do with our current world. You can find these verses in the famous "shoot from the stump of Jesse" passage. It is here that we get a messianic description of what is to come. Some of the text alludes to the story of Jesus here on Earth, and some of it appears to be reserved for the world that lies beyond this one.

People sometimes read this passage and it inspires them to approach small children as miniature gurus. They imply that children can tell us the answers to the world's problems if we just get on their level and *listen*. We hear that children will be the ones to save us from cancer, racism, and global warming.

Of course, this is a lot to ask of them. Especially in a world marked by so much hopelessness and strife. Children will lead us in the next world because, God willing, they will not have been disillusioned by this one yet. They will remind us of a time when the small, sweet tangible things still meant something. They will ask us to go back to that moment when we felt safe.

When our son was born, an elderly friend of ours glanced at the babe in arms and asked me, "When will you tell him how bad the world is?" This was a man who was well into his eighties. He had seen the Depression and served during wartime. He knew hunger and pain intimately. How could we introduce this beautiful little creature to the landscape of sin that the world is? With a mother's defensiveness, I held his small body and said, "The world will do that for us. The world will show him how bad it is." And it has, and it does.

17

WHEN GOD BRINGS THE CHEERIOS

There is a movement afoot in the "Mom World" where we all brag about how awesomely bad we are at parenting. Then we pat each other on the back and try to one-up our fellow mothers' poor decision-making. Over the past few years, I've noticed a similar trend in popular women's theologizing that goes something like this: My life is such a mess. Isn't it great that I own that?

Usually we hold up examples like failed Pinterest projects or our inability to feed our kids anything but chicken nuggets. Such trivialities may indicate petty inabilities but not our more serious *actual problems*. As inconsequential as this may seem, the conversation gets dark, fast.

School sidewalks and playground benches become places for confessing our maternal sin. Only, we do not call it that. We call it "messy." Now, you'll notice, it starts innocently enough. One mom admits to something that's not totally terrible. But instead of just giving her space to admit parental shortcomings, instead of just listening to her, we other mothers jump in and justify our own failures.

(Scene: Morning Drop-Off, 8:04am)

Mom 1: We are so tired! We were up really late letting Johnny watch *PAW Patrol*.

Mom 2: Hey! It happens! We slept in this morning. Susie didn't even get to eat breakfast.

Mom 3: I woke up drunk.

I realize this is a bit of an exaggeration. But there is some truth here as well. We up the ante. And we do so because we do not actually want help. We want to be messy. And while we like to think of this style of parenting as "telling it like it is" or "being honest," I believe it is the opposite.

We are not saying what is *truthfully* happening in our lives. Why was your kid up so late? Why did your daughter miss breakfast? Why the house is never clean? Why do you only eat crappy food? Are you overwhelmed? Depressed? Exhausted? Dealing with marital problems? What are the real sins and issues underneath the surface?

And woe be unto to the mother who does anything intentional and well-meaning for her children. When one of my mom friends crafted homemade valentines for her four-year-old son's class, I found myself chastising her: "Can't you keep the standards low for working mothers? Come on!" I needed some reassurance that my friend didn't have it all together either. Instead of giving her a "Way to Go, Mom!" high-five, I needed her to fail with me, in whatever way I had chosen to define my mess.

Certainly, there are standards of societal judgment that are particularly tough on motherhood. Questions about organic vegetables, academic rigor, and quality time often lead us from one anxious moment to the next. It can all feel like too much.

Which is precisely why being the "Messy Mom" is so appealing. It gives us permission to throw our hands up in the air proclaiming in artsy purple marker "God bless this mess!" as we endure another graceless Bible study on Proverbs 31:10-31. A theology of a "blessed mess" allows us to hide our jealousy, anger, and unresolved hurt in lieu of a carefully crafted monologue about our mess. It is far easier to wave a banner of ineptitude and watch another episode of *Real Housewives*.

Of course, as much as I hate to admit this, nothing real ever happens on the *Real Housewives*. Being genuinely messy means being broken, truly broken, for the world to see. It is not a curated version of our messy life that our souls demand but an honest account of where we need Jesus.

To be clear, I am not advocating for the other extreme. I'm not convinced that the answer lies in some fresh spiritualizing of womanhood. In fact, I'm not sure that God cares about my domestic prowess, one way or the other. Does a sense of my redemption make me long to bake cupcakes with hearts on them? No. But it *does* ground me in an identity that does not depend on me. My identity in Christ cannot be measured in tasks done or left undone, only in the liberating realization that my failure has been recognized and converted into new life.

Some years ago, I was sitting in an undergraduate class with a group of peers who I counted as friends. The Southern Studies Department at Ole Miss is as small as one might imagine. Each individual class felt like its own group of buddies.

On one particular afternoon, class was set to start when we noticed Catherine hadn't shown up yet. Catherine was the kind of person everyone wanted to be friends with. She loved jazz. She lived in an actual house. And, perhaps most exotically, she was a single mother. Per the current culture of motherhood, Catherine was a mess. However, she was also remarkably honest about the challenges she faced, ever earnest and determined to raise her child well.

I would see Catherine around town in Oxford with her three-year-old little girl. I marveled at them. Once, when her daughter was whining in a coffee shop where I worked, Catherine looked at her and said firmly, "Big girl words." This little squeaky voice said to me, "I want a cookie, please!" She was a wonderful mother and an incredibly gifted student. She possessed the kind of commitment to her studies that one only gets from almost losing the chance to get an education at all.

And so when Catherine was late for class, we were all worried. About ten minutes into the lecture, I heard two sets of feet headed toward the classroom. One of them sounded particularly small. Suddenly, Catherine appeared, her face bearing the harried expression of motherhood with which I am so familiar now. Her toddler daughter was at her side, bewildered by our table of undergraduates. I am certain we looked even more surprised to see a small child in our midst.

"I'm so sorry I'm late. The sitter canceled. She'll have to sit with us," Catherine sheepishly announced.

A half-hour went by, and Catherine's daughter began to get restless. Which, of course, made everyone else worried. Especially since none of us appeared equipped to help her. Then, out of nowhere, this beautiful archetype of an Ole Miss sorority girl held up a box and said, "I don't know why I have this. But here's some Honey Nut Cheerios."

To this day, that is the closest thing to a miracle I have ever witnessed. Anyone who has had a fidgety toddler knows that a tiny, random box of Honey Nut Cheerios is not only food, but at least twenty minutes of entertainment.

The rest of us followed suit, rummaging through our

book bags. Slowly but surely, our motley crew helped a mother keep her toddler busy. We passed our car keys down to her. We folded up paper and handed her pens.

Catherine had not presented us with a quirky, "messy" version of motherhood. She didn't come sliding into the classroom like a sitcom character who has had a rough go of being a mommy. She stood before us in urgent need of our help.

Like Catherine—and pretty much all of the mothers I know—I am beyond messy. I am broken and in need of so much help and Good News. If I'm honest, I am ready to see beyond my own bullhockey. I am desperate to pray, "From where is my help to come? My help cometh from the Lord" (Psalm 121:1-2).

In a world where motherly strife and failure seem to revolve around mindless guilt, we can be too consumed with ourselves to face how profoundly we need God. Addictions and anxious tendencies go unaddressed. In our efforts to hide real pain, we deny ourselves (and our fellow mothers) the compassion we desperately need. I wonder if our own sin is just too real for us to handle. I wonder what kind of damage we inflict on ourselves when our story (consciously or not) ends with trivial mess.

The Gospel in all of this, of course, is that God *does* love us no matter how much we long to cling to the mess. That happens *before* we handle our sin and our real difficulties. Cue a sigh of relief.

We have been promised a yoke that is easy and a burden that is light. We are redeemed by a God who asks for whole hearts, not just the parts we want to show. And we are loved by a miracle maker, who shows up in the unlikeliest of places to offer his beloved children (and their mothers) a much-needed box of Cheerios.

18

MARTHA WAS THE WORST

We Christians love to revere the sketchiest figures in the Bible. I am thinking here about people like David (steals a married woman, has her husband killed) or Sarah (insists on abandoning a mother and her baby), and let's not forget Peter (denied Jesus repeatedly). But the queen of misplaced reverence might have to be Martha, the resentful sister we read about in Luke 10:38-42.

People do not want to chastise the lady who is just trying to get the dishes done. I get that. The last thing I want to be told is that my laundry folding is not as valuable as I keep telling myself it is. There are many moments in my day when the only thing that gets me through hand washing a pacifier is the notion that I am doing *the most valuable* work. And while this may get the dishes washed, it also has St. Martha's pathos written all over it.

Churches collectively run to Martha's aid. For a while it was very popular for congregations to have a group of women make casseroles for the sick and needy. Often, these groups would call themselves The Merry Marthas. While I'm all for irresistible puns, one wonders if they've read the passage in question. Did Martha seem "merry" about her King Ranch Casserole? Was she elated to cook up and freeze another vat of Chicken Spaghetti?

Every single time I talk about the story of Mary and Martha, someone tries to educate me on why I need to be more Team Martha. This has happened so many times that I want to plant my flag in the sand: Martha was the worst. She had the messiah in her house, and she decided this was the perfect time to clean and complain. Martha's only defense is that she was the worst because *we* are the worst.

Imagine what it must have been like to have known Jesus the way she did and to have welcomed him into her home for a meal. Mary is not sitting at the feet of a highly regarded teacher; she is sitting at the feet of the messiah himself. And no one wants that seat.

As Pastor Scott Jones once said to me, "Those feet weren't made for dancing—they were made for crucifying." Being in the presence of our Savior means facing your own soul in a way that probably disgusted Martha. Being in the presence of Jesus means giving up on hiding your best-kept secrets: your addiction to booze, porn, and yelling at your kids. Jesus, it turns out, knows about all that stuff. I imagine many of us would rather scrub floors than deal honestly with the mess of our souls.

The spring semester of my second year of seminary I was ready to give up on ordination. Nothing in my life seemed to make any sense. I kept attending classes, reading what was assigned, and feeling exhausted. The overarching message I kept getting was insistent and angry. Time and time again, seminary culture told me I was not doing enough. It felt like everyone had a cause to be outraged about, and if you didn't share the same convictions, or share them strongly enough, you were of no use. I can remember sitting at lunch and just wondering why they didn't just post a big chart on one of the hallway bulletin boards telling us what social injustice we were supposed to be outraged about that week.

Had I been younger and single I would have probably been a better seminarian. I would have shown up for more rallies and had heated debates with classmates about the energy footprint of transporting bananas (seriously). Instead, I started seminary and promptly got pregnant. This decision would change everything for me.

For much of my life I told myself that Jesus needed me in the world working diligently on his behalf. I believed if I really loved him then I would do everything he asked me to do. Only, there is no real Jesus Barometer to measure my works quota. I could never do enough. But based on what I was hearing during my seminary years, Jesus needed me to do *all the things*.

Our son Neil was the first sign that my theology might be askew. He saved me. Babies come into this world adoring their mothers. They are needy and often smelly, sure. But babies love you without your ever having done anything for them. I gave birth over Christmas break my second year of seminary and came back to school a completely different person.

I began ignoring people who tried to make me feel bad about not glomming onto whatever efforts they had deemed important. I was over this notion that Jesus was interested in me signing petitions to save the indigenous peoples of Atlantis. Incidentally, I may have been a bit short-tempered because in my real life I was feeding an adorable baby every two-to-three hours in the evenings.

Part of the reason we make a habit of loving Martha is because she feels so incredibly relatable. Unlike the Biblical trio of David, Sarah, and Peter, Martha does not have a positive story to balance out the bad one we all have written onto our do-gooder hearts. Martha did not rule a nation, she did not birth the people of Israel, and she was not the first leader of the church. Martha was just a woman who did not want to face herself in the light of Jesus. Which is, perhaps, an apt description of most of us.

Jesus tells us in the story that Mary had chosen the "better part." We may nod our heads and mimic agreement with him but, in practice, we all know this is debatable. Sitting at the feet of Jesus sounds like a very difficult way to spend a dinner party. And yet, it is the place where we most belong.

Martha is the Prodigal Daughter of the Gospel. We might like to think of her as the high-accomplishing elder brother in the story, but I give her more credit than that. Just as the Prodigal Son charged toward his father's house, speech in hand, ready to tell him how their relationship would proceed, Martha came at Jesus with her own monologue. She demanded of Jesus, "Lord, do you not care that my sister has left me to serve alone? Tell her then to help me." Jesus assures Martha, "Martha, Martha, you are anxious and troubled by many things." It is clear that Jesus knows Martha even when she has not sat at his feet. He loves her even when she cannot find a way to accept his unmerited grace.

Scripture does not tell us what happened next. But I do not believe Martha heard the words of Christ and kept polishing the silver. I imagine her dishrag and her knees hit the floor at the same moment and she said to Jesus, "You know me. You know how little I bring to your table. And you still want to be with me."

When I hit my lowest point in seminary, I was done doing the dishes. I needed a word of grace spoken profoundly over my life. To put it plainly, I needed Jesus without the agenda of other people. After years of wanting to go to seminary, I hit a point where I did not even care if I got ordained.

Much like Martha, the Prodigal Daughter, I was ready to yell at whoever would listen. The spring I returned to seminary, I plopped down in the library's allegedly quiet computer room and loudly said to a friend of mine, "I cannot take it anymore. I miss my baby constantly. I am so sick of everyone's opinions. I do not want to be here."

Instead of charging back at me with a solid, "I know! Everyone is annoying!" my friend asked me if I had read Paul Zahl's *Grace in Practice*. He told me the Gospel was clear, that we could rest in the forgiveness of sins we had been given. We could find our consolation in the cross. Our work, well intentioned as it is, was not going to be the thing that would save us. Jesus had done that already.

The birth of my son took me down my own path as a Prodigal Daughter, and I never saw it coming. His birth made me long for a kind of unearned grace I desperately needed. In her incredible book, *Traveling Mercies*, Anne Lamott clearly describes what I was looking for:

> It is unearned love—the love that goes before, that greets us on the way. It's the help you receive when you have no bright ideas left, when you are empty and desperate and have discovered that your best thinking and most charming charm have failed you. Grace is the light or electricity or juice or breeze that takes you from that isolated place and puts you with others who are as startled and embarrassed and eventually grateful as you are to be there (139).

That day in the library I heeded my friend's advice. I picked up a copy of PZ's book and signed up for my first Mockingbird Conference in New York City. These two decisions would change almost everything for me. My marriage, my motherhood, my role as a seminarian—basically every avenue of my life began to look radically different. In my third year of seminary, I had finally begun to learn what it meant to be a Christian. I was no longer exhausted by the siren call of self-righteousness. Jesus had saved me even from that.

God willing, we all eventually get tired of running from our Redeemer. We tire of self-justifying, worrying if we have done enough, and obsessing over the work of everyone else. It is there that we find Jesus waiting for us, ready to love us. Like our sister Martha, he beckons us to hold up the dishrag of surrender and say, "Alright, Jesus, I give up. I'll sit down."

19

RON

We were at the rodeo with our kids when we got the news about Ron. One of my husband's old youth group kids called. It felt pretty out of the blue, which are the only type of phone calls Josh tends to answer when he has a day off. When he immediately walked away with the phone clenched to his ear, I knew it was bad.

I was standing there with our two kids who were very excited to be surrounded by the rodeo hubbub. I took a deep breath and tried to keep them distracted. As Josh approached us, I just blurted out, "It's Ron, isn't it? He's killed himself?"

We had known Ron for a very long time. He was a parishioner at Josh's first church in Georgia. Ron had a huge personality. He could be loving, generous, hilarious, and entirely offensive all in the same conversation. Once, when Josh and I were still dating, Ron emceed an auction at my husband's church where he shamed the entire audience to keep them from bidding against Josh. There were some very expensive pearls on the block, and Josh was bidding against a parishioner. In the middle of bidding, Ron held up his hand to signal that the parishioner needed to stop raising his paddle and said, "Let the young priest get the pearls for his girlfriend. You know he doesn't make much money." That was a classic Ron move: loud, gracious, and aggressive.

Ron was the kind of guy that people described as being "larger than life." Those words would ring repeatedly in my head the morning we found out he had killed himself. We knew Ron's personal life had been difficult, and we knew Ron himself could be difficult. We wondered (and feared) if that would be a lethal combination for him.

Every time we hear of a suicide, questions quickly follow. Normally, these inquiries are laden with a kind of judgment about how selfish it is to kill yourself. How could you just leave everyone behind with your problems to solve? Why is it up to you to say when your life ends?

As a teenager in the Bible Belt South, I can remember the discussions of Hell that always followed suicide. I was very quiet in those moments. It felt like people were talking about the wrong issue. They did not care about what haunted the person who took their own life. Instead, they wanted to know if death at your own hand was a one-way ticket to Satanville.

My grandfather shot himself in the head when my Mom was a toddler. From all accounts, Woodrow Ferguson was also "larger than life." The descriptions of him never fit the expectations of a young man growing up dirt poor in the deep South. He rode a motorcycle cross-country with my grandmother. He amassed an impressive collection of classical music records. I am told that when he and his friends would skin deer during the hunting season, my grandfather would stand next to the deer's carcass with a book about animal anatomy. Basically, he was my kind of weird.

But I know the other stories, too. I know that he was in and out of military psychiatric hospitals for much of my grandparents' marriage. I know that in his manic episodes, he used to gather the family on their knees for fervent prayer with talk of being missionaries and leaving it all behind. I know he struggled profoundly with feeling he was never going to be good enough. And, perhaps most heartbreakingly, I know he shot himself in 1955 when psychiatric medicine was just on the cusp of devising breakthrough drugs which could have dramatically improved his mental state.

Perhaps that is why I find it very difficult to hear of a suicide and feel anything except sadness and empathy. I say this as someone who has seen the unholy horror that remains behind when suicide happens. I have seen my mother walk through the hardest questions and the most profound abandonment imaginable. I grew up sitting at the kitchen table with my grandmother who had only stories of struggle and grief in the years that followed Woodrow's suicide. Even decades after his death, my grand-mother would avoid running into people in town. I often wondered if it was because she worried that just seeing her face would remind them of all that she had been through, and she simply could not bear the burden all over again. The financial, emotional, and spiritual ramifications of suicide are far from lost on me. If someone kills them-selves, their pain will echo in a family for generations.

In the aftermath of suicide, we tend to postulate that the individual should have remembered their family and more thoughtfully considered the pain their death would cause. Aren't your family and friends enough to stay alive for? When Ron died, I remember being struck by the hun-dreds of people who showed up to mourn him. I couldn't help but wonder, "What would have happened if we had all just shown up to be with Ron when he was alive?" But, of course, so many people did.

People *had* tried to reach out. The church had been very involved in helping him. The truth of the matter is that even if we had all come to Ron's aid for a few days, he still would have been left with his misunderstood pain and forlornness. I am convinced Ron was determined his life should end in this way. I do not think we could have stopped it.

We are quick to forget that when people choose to kill themselves, they feel entirely out of choices. Notes from the dead opine, "You'll be better off without me." People who kill themselves are working under a distorted view of selflessness. Which just makes the pain of their loss even more profound.

Losses like these are always followed by an ocean of anger, devastation, and endless questions. We do not know what it is like to be so haunted by the world that we can no longer live in it. We cannot guess at what is happening in someone else's head. And yet, if you have lost someone you love to this terrible phenomenon, then you know the endless mental exercises you will suffer trying to figure out the unknowable.

Over the years, the church has offered little comfort to those left behind. At best, preachers have said nothing about suicide. At worst, they have made guesses about what the afterlife must hold for a person who is willing to take away the gift of life God has given them. For years, I never found consolation for suicide in the church. But finally, Martin Luther offered me some.

There's a scene in the movie *Luther* that depicts a legend from early in Martin Luther's ministry. A young man in his parish has hung himself and his parents are in unthinkable grief. Immediately, Luther finds the man's hanging body, cuts it down himself, and takes him to the church graveyard to be buried. Of course, church tradition had long prohibited the bodies of those who had committed suicide from being laid to rest in consecrated property. In the movie, the grave keeper insists to Martin, "The boy is damned! I am not allowed to do this! The others won't rest with him in here! This is holy ground!"

In an act of total pastoral devotion, Martin digs the grave in the churchyard himself. As his parishioners stare aghast at what he is doing, he says to them, "Some people say that according to God's justice this boy is damned because he took his own life. I say he was overcome by the devil. Is this child any more to blame for the despair that overtook him than the innocent man who was murdered by a robber in the woods?"

What comfort those few moments of a movie have given me. I always believed what he said was true. In those quiet moments as a child when people would insist suicide was selfish, immature, and punishable, I always knew they were missing something. The *Luther* scene confirmed that God's grace operates in the least expected ways to rescue the lonely from themselves. It was the comforting words that I had always given myself but never heard aloud.

In human terms, it makes sense that people who have taken their own lives should have to go to hell. After all, they have neglected their earthly responsibilities and irrevocably damaged their families. They have presumed an authority over life and death which belongs to God. They have hated themselves to the point of no return.

Biblically speaking, I never hear the Parable of the Ninety-Nine Sheep without thinking about suicide. There is no clearer vision of God seeking out the lost among us. It is totally ridiculous. Why would the shepherd go to find this one wandering off into the wilderness? Shouldn't he want to stay with the rule-following sheep? The ones who die of natural causes? The ones who are grateful for the life they have been given? It is easier to just write off the lost ones, assuming they never want to be found. In a sermon on this parable, theologian Gerhard Forde once preached:

> But if there is peril in leaving the ninety-nine in their scandalized bitterness, perhaps that is not even half the battle. For what of the one upon whom all this attention is lavished? Are there not endless possibilities for offense there too? It could be, could it not, that the one doesn't even know or care that it is lost?[9]

I love this take on the parable. God seeks out the most offensively lost among us. He desires to care for those who might not even want to be found. Of course, we are all too often the lost sheep ourselves. The spectrum of loneliness and depression is not as black-and-white as we might like to think.

When someone we love takes his or her own life, we are left with an unquenchable sadness and unanswerable questions. But I trust God in this and not my own anxious heart. I trust that when people find this world so undoable that they become undone by it, God does not aban-

---

9. From Forde's incredible sermon "The Perilous Journey," found on pages 99-101 of his book, *The Captivation of the Will: Luther vs. Erasmus on Freedom and Bondage.*

don them. He seeks out the Rons and Woodrows in our lives. He tucks them so deeply into his heart that those who doubted his profound love for them would know it profoundly.

20

THE OLD, OLD STORY
THAT TURNS THE CHURCH AROUND

The night Josh was made rector of a church[10] for the first time was the proudest I have ever been as a priest's wife. We had been married for four years, were still childless, and had loads of ego to go around. When our bishop came to preach and officially put Josh in charge, I remember being ready to absorb all of the encouraging "You can do it! Yes you can!" that he was going to cheerlead our way.

Instead, he stood in the pulpit and spoke about how difficult it is to turn a ship around, literally. There were some very specific nautical details and an unbelievably long timeline. Apparently, if the ship is big enough, and the water is rough enough, it can take days, even a week, to turn a ship around. This was not the victory-in-leadership sermon I had been hoping for.

The bishop went on to explain that Josh could not

---

10. Head priest/pastor/person in charge of keeping the lights on.

singlehandedly turn his church in a brand-new direction. He told us that it would take more than simply Josh's ideas and brave heart to get the job done. We would need church leadership that wanted to see change. We would need people in the pews who were prepared to rally behind the new rector. Yet, even with all of that, the bishop suggested, we could still fail. "God is going to do what God is going to do here," he told us.

I felt so many emotions at that service. Initially, I remember being angry with the bishop. He should have come in and told everyone Josh was going to save the church. The anger was short-lived, though. I knew the bishop was right. My immature frustration quickly shifted into relief.

The truth was, and is, and always has been, that it is not up to us to fix the state of the church. It is up to us to tell the Gospel story. Whatever comes from that is beyond our control.

There is an anxiety that pulses through our churches these days about empty pews and shrinking budgets. We are looking for someone to save us from despair. But our anguish is misplaced. Instead of looking to the world and seeing the hurting wash of humanity, we look to our churches and worry that we cannot maintain our current way of doing things. We speculate that it may take an entire group of people to save us. We need cooler people, younger people, and/or richer people.

My friend, the Reverend Jacob Smith, tells a story

about attending an ecumenical pastors' group in New York City. The clergy were asked to share who the "target audience" was for their individual churches. One by one, each clergy person responded that their church was interested in adding more young people and artists to their respective congregations. When it came around to Jacob, he said, "We'd like to get more middle-aged divorced women." It was a funny and pointed way to remind the other clergy that churches are not intended to be places where people go to feel more hip. Churches are places where the Gospel binds up the brokenhearted.

Seminary was full of conversations like my friend Jacob experienced. We were always talking about *who* we were interested in doing ministry *for*. Who was our focus group for Jesus going to be? Do we want to minister to millennials, to nerds, or perhaps to nerdy millennials? Are we all going to plant inner city community gardens? Should we focus our ministries on purple aliens from the Southern hemisphere of Mars?

When the subject of vocation is broached, people often quote a famous Frederick Buechner line: "The place you're called to is the place where your deep gladness and the world's deep hunger meet." In mainline Christian churches and seminaries, we tend to throw quotes like this around as if they were the words of Jesus himself. The church has a habit of making such mantras sacrosanct. The result being that we cannot question what they mean or how we may be destructively using them.

In the case of Frederick Buchner, who is a wonderful theologian, this quote is often hauled out of the secular scripture songbook when we want to take on a ministry that we have deemed meaningful and worthy of our attention. Professors in seminary would often ask us, "What is it that YOU want to do?" As though that were the only qualifier for God's work in the world.

Imagine what the Gospel would have looked like if Jesus had encountered each of his disciples and asked them, "What is it that YOU want to do? What are YOUR personal interests? What ideas do YOU have for my church?" We would have had stories about guys who opened a stinky fish shop where you can also get your taxes done.

Fortunately, Jesus did not care what people's personal interests were. He did not care whether or not they felt like they brought "something" to the table. Because Jesus knew that our deepest gladness is only ever one thing: God's word of forgiveness spoken over our sinful hearts. Anything else will fall short.

The fact of the matter is that most of our ideas about how to fix the church are terrible, my own included. We over-exaggerate what we can do, and we forget that nothing happens that has not first been named by God. We figure that our ministry *de jour* will grow the church, because we love our latest idea, and if we love it, how can anything be wrong? Well, if *we* love it, then everything can be wrong with it.

All of this makes for anxious pastors leading anxious

churches. When we do not care about the ancient of days God who we worship, when we fail to see his hand guiding us, then we have only ourselves, our egos, and our interests to fall back on.

I believe this description applies to a great many of our churches: nice places, full of kind people, who are told, Sunday after Sunday, that they need to bring more people to church or do more work for Jesus. It can feel like scrambling to please an absentee parent. Our anxious hearts silently suffer, all the while trying desperately to do more and be more for God Almighty.

In our "turn this ship around" determinations, I wonder if we do not unintentionally place God in the role of an uncaring father. Like the disciples in the boat (Luke 8: 23-27), perhaps we wonder if God even cares if we drown? If we're as able-bodied and brilliant as we claim to be, one begins to wonder if we truly need God in the church at all?

I worry that, in all our efforts to meet God in the middle or to outreach our way to the stars, we have missed the point of the Gospel. If the Gospel is only about what I am interested in or what I bring to the table, then perhaps we should abandon the whole enterprise altogether. When I look at the rapidly declining state of Christianity, of the church, I cannot help but wonder if that is already slowly happening. In a desperate desire to save an institution, are we forsaking God?

Then a very depressing thought follows, "I wonder if

the church's decline makes God happy or sad."

I know that it makes *me* very sad. Because the church is so much more than our pitiful contributions. The church is so much more than our pet causes and political agendas. The church is the Bride of Christ, adulterous though she may be. And we are her very fortunate servants.

In the middle of our self-aggrandizing talk about Biblical scholarship, or our very bad ideas for how to run Vacation Bible School, stands an institution on which we are privileged to hang our hats. The church is Jesus's one clear stake in the world. She is here to blanket the world with talk of his unrelenting forgiveness, to take his message of love to the least, the lost, and the lonely. The church does not need our insights about what is the most interesting or most current opinion. She needs our hearts.

The nineteenth-century pastor, the Rev. Dr. Stephen Tyng, had served in ordained ministry for fifty years when he was asked to deliver a series of lectures to the School of Theology at Boston University. His subject matter was "The Christian Pastor," and he spoke about, among other things, the task of preaching. I return to one portion of his remarks on a weekly basis. When ministry feels tedious, Tyng reminds us that God is for the brokenhearted. And when ministry feels insufferable, Tyng reminds us that we are among them:

> This is your message to each, to all to whom you are sent. It is "the old, old, story," yet it is always

new, always living, and by God's Holy Spirit always to be made effectual. Wherever we go, we have the same great and gracious message committed to us; and we "are not ashamed of the Gospel of Christ, the power of God unto salvation to everyone who believeth." We love to tell this precious story—over, over, and over again—[at] every house, at every bedside of sickness; in every chamber of sorrow; to every anxious, burdened heart, in the midst of every afflicted household, to every waiting sinner like ourselves, wherever we may find him.

We are never wearied with proclaiming this gracious message from God. We love to repeat this effective intelligence of pardon for the chief of sinners, through the atoning blood of an Almighty Savior.[11]

The old, old story that Tyng references has nothing to do with a pastor turning the ship of the church around. He did not stand in front of a room full of seminarians and tell them that the future of the church was about their personal interests or how many young people they could get through the doors. He told them that their job was to preach a word of grace over God's people again and again and again.

The message of the Gospel is the same thing it has always been. It is about Jesus Christ who stood on the boat

---

11. *The Office and Duty of a Christian Pastor* (Harper & Brothers, 1874), 21-22.

with his beloved, sinful friends and said, "I will calm the storms of your life. I will rescue you from yourselves. I will speak a word of pardon over your weary, sinsick souls." That is the Gospel.

Today, my husband and I are fifteen years into a life of ministry. We do not talk with the same bravado we once did. We do not marvel at our "incredible talents" any more. We marvel that God lets us do this incredible work at all.

There is enormous relief to be found here. It is not on us to turn the ship around. God is going to do what God is going to do. And it is certainly not on us to save anyone. Jesus already has. Our job is simply to tell that wonderful old, old story on repeat.

21

A WORD OVER US

In 2013 the *Harvard Business Review* published a study called "If Your Boss Thinks You're Awesome, You Will Become Awesome." Their research proved what every low (wo)man on the totem pole already knew: If your boss treats you like a great employee, it will make you less likely to be a bad one. Results showed the quality of peoples' leadership within a company being vastly better if their boss believed that they were, in fact, awesome. Conversely, the harder your bosses are on you, the less effective your work and leadership were in the eyes of your peers. In other words, if your boss speaks a word of worthiness over you, you begin to believe you are worthy.

Most of us have work experience that speaks to this dichotomy. In my first grown-up job, I had a boss who would stand at the door every day and tell me if I was late. Most mornings I was not. And so she would begrudgingly grumble out a "Good morning, Sarah." However, when I was running behind she would bark out, "TWO MIN-UTES LATE!" to me at the door followed by a "You're lucky we are so forgiving!"

Forgiving indeed.

The thing about that job was that I enjoyed most of it. I was basically the doorman of the institution. I got to meet all kinds of people. I answered the phone. There was free coffee. What was not to love?

Well, regularly being told that I was inadequate wore on me. Eventually, certain spreadsheets went undone. I would occasionally just ignore a phone call. Towards the end, when I knew I was leaving, I would show up late just to spite my supervisor. She seemed to think I was a steaming pile of crap so I figured I might as well fulfill her expectations.

When I got the phone call to interview for my first job as a parish priest, I remember thinking that the guy who wanted to hire me was insane. I was thirty-seven weeks pregnant, and I had exactly one pair of pants that still fit me. When I told him that I would not officially start working until four months after the baby was born he replied, "Sounds good! Everyone is excited!" When I told him that I only wanted to come in one day a week to start he said, "Great! We will be happy to have you." As you might imagine, this only made him seem crazier.

What I did not realize was that his open-hearted en-couragement was a sign of the kind of employment I was entering. It is a graceful place, full of forgiveness. Consequently, I have never worked harder at a job, nor have I loved a job more. No one has ever chastised me for my timeliness or belittled me over anything. I stay later than is required. I take on basically every project that gets offered to me. I always pick up the phone.

None of this is because I am a better person than I was at my first job. It is because righteousness was imputed to me. I was told I was beloved and worthy and so I began to believe it and act accordingly.

The imputed righteousness of Christ sounds like one of those theological terms that you should have an advanced degree to make sense of. Do not let that dissuade you from engaging with it. Imputation is a concept you have born witness to over and over again. In its plainest terms, we are made righteous through the righteousness of Christ. In *Harvard Business Review* terms, our boss thinks we are awesome.

You have seen imputation at work with your spouse, your family, and perhaps especially, with your children. Whether we realize it or not, we are always speaking a word of worthiness or unworthiness, forgiveness or guilt, good or bad, over our kids. They look to us all the time to tell them that they are beloved.

Our son has a request he makes most nights of the week when I kiss him goodnight. He asks me to tell him "Stories from When I Was a Walking Baby in Du Nork," which translates to "stories he remembers from being a toddler in New York." They are little glimpses into his early years. He wants to hear about when he first learned to walk or about how he liked to "pet the brie" at fancy parties we would throw at the rectory. Mostly, I feel like he wants to hear about the time in his life when a word of grace and love were spoken over him. He wants the song of his imputed worthiness to be the last thing he hears before going to sleep.

To be honest, as his mother, I need to be reminded of it, too. Even small children have people watching for them to step out of line. In fact, they are perhaps worse off than the rest of us. Behavior charts and rules galore are a fixture in their daily lives. Realistically, there are expectations they cannot meet and rules they will refuse to follow.

As a parent, it becomes easy to impute "badly be-haved" onto them. Our anxiety about raising law-abiding citizens can cause us to say terrible things to our children and to act as though their sin defines who they are. Of course, this never helps.

They simply need to have love spoken over their hearts despite the lack of stickers in their "I Had a Good Day" school report. As a mother, I must remember that my love for them was there long before they could earn or do any-thing right. When the doctor placed our newborn son in my arms, I believed he was beauty incarnate. Remember-ing that, speaking that truth over him, imputes a kind of worthiness that no amount of "You can do it, kiddo!" could ever do. When we look at our children and only see the anxiety of a bad note from school or their failure to keep up in soccer practice, we treat them like they have fallen from grace. When, through Jesus Christ, nothing could be further from the truth.

Marriage can feel like ground zero for the power of imputation. When we look at our spouses and see someone who fails to meet our standards, we treat them like trash. We complain and subtly let them know that they are not measuring up.

Marriage advice articles are always asserting that we should retell the stories of how we first met and fell in love. Where were we when that happened? How did we feel before the arguments about money and unloading the dishwasher began? How light did our hearts feel when all was forgiven so easily? I have noticed that after particularly difficult weeks when my husband and I feel compelled to order in sushi (sans salmon) and share a bottle of wine, we will whisper to one another, "Remember how you proposed in the kitchen? Remember how we cried?" We long to remind ourselves of the imputed love we saw in one another.

Often in one of those stressful, late evening arguments, we can access a long list of things we allegedly loathe about one other. The shift that happens in these fights always alarms me. If my husband tells me I seem impatient or edgy I will think to myself, "CHALLENGE ACCEPTED." Thankfully, over the years he has developed the habit of saying, "Hey Sweet Lady" before he says anything else. He is not denying me of anger or telling me we cannot fight, he is simply saying, "You are kind. Can we speak love over one another?"

The imputation of Christ goes far beyond anything *we* can give. Jesus gave us his righteousness. Full stop. No questions asked. We hear in 2 Corinthians 6:21, "God made him who had no sin to be sin for us, so that in him we might become the righteousness of God." Which is to say, Jesus came to save us from our sin, to take the weight of our sin on himself, so that we would be made righteous in the sight of our Maker.

It is worth noting that the Devil will impute horrible things to those we love and to us. In moments of deep pain and sin, he will lean in and whisper, "Not good enough. Will never measure up. Needs more work." This line of thought will get into your bones and impute only desperate loneliness. The imputation of Jesus Christ speaks a word over us that says, "righteous, beloved, and forgiven." We are made holy through his holiness, and we cannot let evil tell us otherwise. I cannot pray these words from Martin Luther enough:

> So when the devil throws your sins in your face and declares that you deserve death and hell, tell him this: "I admit that I deserve death and hell, what of it? For I know One who suffered and made satisfaction on my behalf. His name is Jesus Christ, Son of God, and where He is there I shall be also!"

Most of us do not want to admit that we are constantly searching for a word of some sort to be spoken over our lives. We want to know whether or not we have done a "good job." We tirelessly strive to impress the rest of humanity. Sometimes we luck out in this life and are surrounded by people who encourage us and offer us grace. Other times, though, we can feel no firm ground beneath us. Our boss may be one of the most inspiring people we have had the opportunity to work for. Or, we can feel as though we have been employed by a Disney villain.

The incredible part of imputation is that our worthiness does not have to rely on the whims of our fellow human beings. In fact, it does not even fall into the category of our personal responsibility. Jesus has imputed his righteousness to us. And this changes everything.

There is no "magic switch" in Christianity which somehow makes us better people. Yet, the imputation of Jesus makes us see the world in a powerfully different way. We were irredeemable and yet have been redeemed. We were always late, and yet, are always on time. We once were lost but have been found.

When Jesus Christ died for our sins, he became the Word of righteousness in our stead.

We long for a God who will not count our sin against us. It is no wonder that employees, employers, wives, husbands, and sweet little kindergarteners are all longing for a word of righteousness to be spoken over their lives. Our souls are searching for a savior who can call us by name and tell us we are worthy and beloved.

In Jesus Christ that is exactly what we have found.

Or, I should say, has found us.

ABOUT MOCKINGBIRD

Founded in 2007, Mockingbird is an organization devoted to connecting the Christian faith with the realities of everyday life in fresh and down-to-earth ways. We do this primarily, but not exclusively, through conferences, publications, and online resources. To find out more, visit us at www.mbird.com.

ALSO FROM MOCKINGBIRD

The Mockingbird Quarterly
edited by Ethan Richardson

More Theology & Less Heavy Cream
by Robert Farrar Capon

Mockingbird at the Movies
edited by C.J. Green and David Peterson

Law and Gospel: A Theology for Sinners (and Saints)
by Will McDavid, Ethan Richardson, and David Zahl

A Mess of Help:
From the Crucified Soul of Rock N'Roll
by David Zahl

Eden and Afterward: A Mockingbird Guide to Genesis
by Will McDavid

PZ's Panopticon:
An Off-the-Wall Guide to World Religion
by Paul F.M. Zahl

The Mockingbird Devotional:
Good News for Today (and Everyday)
edited by Ethan Richardson and Sean Norris

Grace in Addiction:
The Good News of Alcoholics Anonymous for Everybody
by John Z.

This American Gospel:
Public Radio Parables and the Grace of God
by Ethan Richardson

*Our books are available at www.mbird.com/publications
or on Amazon, and our quarterly magazine can be found
at magazine.mbird.com.*

Made in the USA
Columbia, SC
09 March 2021